TWAYNE'S WORLD AUTHORS SERIES

A Survey of the World's Literature

Sylvia E. Bowman, Indiana University

GENERAL EDITOR

SPAIN

Janet W. Díaz, University of North Carolina, Chapel Hill

EDITOR

The Duke of Rivas

TWAS 452

The Duke of Rivas

THE DUKE OF RIVAS

By GABRIEL LOVETT

TWAYNE PUBLISHERS

A DIVISION OF G. K. HALL & CO., BOSTON

Library of Congress Cataloging in Publication Data

Lovett, Gabriel H
    The Duke of Rivas.

    (Twayne's world authors series ; TWAS 452 : Spain)
    Bibliography: pp. 179–85
    Includes index.
    1. Rivas, Angel Pérez de Saavedra Ramírez de Madrid
Remírez de Baquedano, duque de, 1791–1865–Criticism and
interpretation. I. Title.
PQ6560.Z5L64   868′.5′09   77–5136
ISBN 0–8057–6289–2

MANUFACTURED IN THE UNITED STATES OF AMERICA

To Patricia

Contents

About the Author

Gabriel Lovett was born in Berlin and lived in Germany and France before coming to the United States in 1939. He received the B.A., M.A., and Ph.D. degrees from New York University. Professor Lovett taught at New York University and Monmouth College. He directed the New York University in Spain Program from 1960 to 1965. After his return to this country, he became chairman of the Spanish department at NYU. In 1969 he left New York to join the faculty at Wellesley College, serving as Chairman of the Spanish Department there from 1970 to 1975. He currently teaches Spanish and history of the Hispanic world at Wellesley. His works include *Napoleon and the Birth of Modern Spain* (New York, 1965).

Preface

Angel de Saavedra, Duke of Rivas, is too often known, in Spain as well as abroad, only because of his super-Romantic play *Don Alvaro o la fuerza del sino* (*Don Alvaro or the Power of Fate*). While *Don Alvaro* is an important contribution to Spanish Romanticism, it should not obscure Rivas' other literary accomplishments, which are considerable. His *El moro expósito* (*The Foundling Moor*) stands as a solid achievement in the field of narrative poetry, and his historical ballads must be considered among the best of this traditional and most Spanish genre of poetry. His great talent as a narrative poet makes him one of the outstanding, as well as one of the more representative, figures of Spanish Romanticism.

I have analyzed all the important works as well as less important material such as the later lyrics and the prose sketches which contain some compositions that deserve comment. The analysis follows a chronological order as far as possible. In the first chapter, devoted to the life and times of Rivas, I have included a section on Spanish Romanticism to help the reader place Rivas' work in clearer perspective.

This study does not contain a separate chapter on Rivas' aesthetics simply because the Duke, though well aware of what he was doing and certainly not devoid of aesthetic ideas, did not generally choose to express his views on these matters. The most important essay in this respect is the preface to *El moro expósito*, which, while having doubtless received Rivas' approval, was not written by him but by his friend Antonio Alcalá Galiano. At the beginning of Chapter 3 I have devoted some space to this preface, which is considered almost a manifesto of Spanish Romanticism. I have also examined Rivas' own most important statement concerning aesthetic matters, the prologue to his *Romances históricos* (*Historical Ballads*), in which he praises the Spanish ballad and ballad meter. My comments on this passage are found at the beginning of Chapter 5. In speeches to the Royal Spanish Academy, as well as in some prologues, there are a few more pronouncements concerning the Spanish language and the novel, but they are not important enough to warrant separate treatment.

I have used the poet's family name Saavedra for the period of his life before he actually inherited the title of Duke of Rivas in 1834, and the title name Rivas for his work following this moment in his life. Although usage by previous writers on this point varies, it seems to me that this is a more logical procedure than adopting the title name from the very beginning, when the young Saavedra was not yet Duke.

I have taken my quotations mostly from the three-volume edition of Rivas' work by Jorge Campos in the *Biblioteca de Autores Españoles* (1957) which, though containing quite a few printing errors, is the most complete edition available at present. When a volume is alluded to for the first time in a chapter, it is so indicated in a note. Subsequent quotations from the same volume are identified in parentheses following the original phrasing.

I wish to express my deep appreciation to the family of the late Professor Nicholson B. Adams and to Professor Janet W. Díaz of the University of North Carolina at Chapel Hill for letting me have Dr. Adams' notes on the Duke of Rivas. The notes were to have been part of a study on this author. Chapter 2 owes much to the notes, and some material of Chapter 3 is also based on them.

GABRIEL LOVETT

Chronology

1791   March 10: Angel de Saavedra is born in Cordova.
1803   Enters the Real Seminario de Nobles in Madrid.
1806   Enters the Royal Guards. Date of his earliest known poem.
1809   November 18: Gravely wounded in battle of Ontígola against French.
1810   Works for the general staff of the Spanish army in Cádiz; promoted to rank of captain.
1814   Publishes volume of poetry which contains 30 short compositions as well as *El paso honroso*.
1814– Writes a number of tragedies in the Neoclassic manner.
1818
1821   December: Elected deputy for Cordova to the new liberal Cortes in Madrid.
1820– Second edition of poems; many additions to the poems
1821   of 1814.
1822   Writes the tragedy *Lanuza*, which is performed before enthusiastic audiences.
1823   October 3: Forced to flee to Gibraltar.
1824- Sojourn in London. Begins to work on narrative poem
1825   *Florinda*.
1825   In Gibraltar marries María de la Encarnación de Cueto y Ortega. The couple arrives in Malta, where Saavedra meets John Hookham Frere.
1826   Completion of *Florinda*.
1827   Composition of tragedy *Arias Gonzalo*.
1828   Composition of *Tanto vales cuanto tienes* and "El faro de Malta."
1829   September: Begins composition of *El moro expósito*.
1830– Residence in France. *Don Alvaro* written in Tours in
1834   1832. *El moro expósito* completed in Paris in 1833; published in 1834.

1834 January: Returns to Spain. May: Upon death of older brother inherits the title of Duke of Rivas. October: Becomes member of Royal Spanish Academy.

1835 March 22: Performance of *Don Alvaro*.

1836 Forced to take refuge in Gibraltar.

1837 August: Returns to Spain.

1840– Residence in Seville.
1843

1841 Publication of *Romances históricos*.

1841– Publication of *Solaces de un prisionero, La morisca de*
1842 *Alajuar,* and *El crisol de la lealtad.*

1844 Publication of *El desengaño en un sueño* and *El parador de Bailén.*

1844– Serves as Minister Plenipotentiary and Ambassador at
1850 Court of Naples.

1854 July: Appointed Prime Minister and Secretary of the Navy (40 hours).

1854– Publication of collected works in five volumes.
1855

1857– Serves as Ambassador in Paris.
1858

1862 February: Elected Director of the Royal Spanish Academy.

1865 June 22: Dies in Madrid.

CHAPTER 1

The Life and Times of Rivas

I The Early Years

THE future Duke of Rivas was born Angel Pérez de Saavedra in Cordova on March 10, 1791. He was the second son of the grandees of Spain Don Juan Martín de Saavedra y Ramírez Pérez y Saavedra, Duke of Rivas, and Doña María Dominga Remírez de Baquedano y Quiñones, Marquise of Andía and Villasinda. Like many other boys of well-to-do families, Angel received his early education from French clerics who had fled the French Revolution and sought refuge in Spain. In Cordova he was taught history, geography, and French by a Monsieur Tostín; after his family had moved to Madrid because of a yellow fever epidemic, he was given lessons by two other French émigrés residing in the capital.

From an early age Angel showed great interest and talent in poetry and painting. "Don Angel Saavedra was a painter and a poet from his days in the cradle," writes his biographer Nicomedes Pastor Díaz.[1] His love for poetry was no doubt encouraged by his father, who himself was a versifier of sorts; his affection for art, particularly drawing, was spurred by a French sculptor, Monsieur Verdiguier, residing in Cordova. From an early age, too, Angel developed a fierce love for his native Andalusia and for his birthplace Cordova, which was to show itself time and again in his work. While in Madrid as a child, he no doubt missed the south and wished he were back in the Andalusian sunshine on the banks of the Guadalquivir.

When he was eleven, Angel de Saavedra's father died, and the older son, Juan Remigio, became Duke of Rivas. Angel was sent to the Real Seminario de Nobles (Royal Seminary for Noblemen) in Madrid, where he continued his studies.[2] Poetry and history were his favorite subjects, while science bored him. Even then he was composing verse of some merit which tried to imitate the great sixteenth-century poet Fernando de Herrera (1534–97); at the same time he was translating Latin classics into good Spanish verse.

These were eventful years. Spain, on the decline as a great power ever since the death of Charles III (1759–88), had become a satellite of Napoleon Bonaparte and in 1804 became involved in renewed war against England on the side of France. This war brought Spain among other things the terrible naval disaster of Trafalgar (1805). Charles IV (1788–1808) was king but let his favorite, Manuel Godoy, govern in his stead. Godoy tried desperately to please Napoleon and at the same time neutralize his many enemies within Spain, among whom the most dangerous was the royal heir Ferdinand, who was regarded by many Spaniards as the potential savior of the country.

II *Military Service, War, and Political Turmoil*

In 1806, Angel de Saavedra joined the Royal Guards and in the service made friends with a group of young men who edited a journal. The future Duke wrote prose articles and verse for it, and at least some of these compositions found their way into his first collection of poems, which was to come out in 1814. But times were not to be too propitious for literary activities. Napoleon introduced his troops into northern Spain with the aim of occupying Portugal. This aim was achieved by the end of 1807, but the French troops remained in Spain and also occupied Madrid. In the meantime a popular revolt had overthrown Godoy and forced Charles IV to abdicate. Ferdinand was the new king, but not for long. Napoleon invited him to join him at Bayonne in southern France; once the young monarch had arrived there, he was held prisoner and forced to relinquish the Spanish crown. Napoleon thought that by placing this crown on the head of his brother Joseph he would have Spain firmly in his grasp and would transform the ramshackle Spanish monarchy into a powerful ally in his war against England. But the French emperor had not taken into account the reaction of the Spanish people. Large areas of Spain revolted against the French and thus began the ferocious Spanish War of Independence (1808–14) which was to fatally undermine Napoleon's empire.

Don Angel, beside his brother the Duke, fought with the rank of lieutenant against Napoleon and took part in several battles. In one of these, at Ontígola, south of Madrid, on November 18, 1809, Saavedra lost his horse, fought on foot, and was so severely wounded that he was left for dead. A Spanish soldier found him and took him to a nearby town, where, in a private home, a surgeon tended his wounds. His brother had him evacuated and Angel was sent to a hospital in the Andalusian town of Baeza, where he composed the famous ballad which begins with the words "Con once heridas mortales" ("With eleven mortal wounds").

From Baeza Angel traveled to Cordova, where he continued his recovery from his wounds. But Andalusia was doomed. The French armies, shortly after their crushing victory at Ocaña, crashed through the barrier of the Sierra Morena in January, 1810, and rapidly occupied most of the southern province. Angel fled to Málaga with his mother and from there to Gibraltar. Finally he was able to reach Cádiz, which for more than two years was to resist the onslaught of the French enemy. In Cádiz, promoted to the rank of captain and later to that of lieutenant colonel, he obtained a position on the general staff of the army and soon became editor of the official staff journal. He also continued to write poetry, inspired no doubt by the example of his new-found friends also residing in Cádiz at the time: the poets Juan Nicasio Gallego, Juan Bautista Arriaza, and especially the great patriotic bard Manuel José Quintana (1772–1857), who in his Neoclassic compositions had extolled liberty and preached all-out resistance to the invaders.[3]

It was in Cádiz that Saavedra composed his first long poem, *El paso honroso* (*The Passage at Arms*; 1812) and a number of other poems in the Neoclassic manner which were soon to have a wider audience. But military affairs and poetry were not the only things keeping the young man busy. There was political turmoil in the great seaport. Liberalism was winning the day in the national Cortes or Parliament which was then meeting in Cádiz. A liberal constitution, signifying an important break with Spain's absolutist past, was promulgated in 1812, and Saavedra was among the enthusiastic supporters of the new ideas. By 1814 the war with France was over. The French had been driven from Spain and Napoleon dethroned. The War of Independence left a strong imprint on Rivas. The intense nationalism which we find in his poetic compositions, and which increased as he grew older, can be traced to some extent to the years 1808–1814, as can the Francophobia which we find from time to time in his work.

When Ferdinand VII returned from exile in 1814, he abolished the constitution and the liberal reforms, and jailed many liberals. Strangely enough, no measures were taken against Saavedra. In fact, he was given a post in Seville and later promoted (1816) from the rank of lieutenant colonel to that of colonel. In 1814 he published a volume of poetry which contained thirty short compositions as well as *El paso honroso*. In the same year he wrote a Neoclassic tragedy in five acts called *Ataúlfo* which was prohibited by the censor. Other tragedies followed and were staged in several towns with moderate success. He also wrote lyric poetry dealing mostly with love, including the intense compositions addressed to a lady called Olimpia which date from 1819 and 1820.

In this latter year a revolution, promoted mainly by liberal elements in the army, forced King Ferdinand VII to swear allegiance to the constitution of 1812. Saavedra enthusiastically joined the ranks of the revolutionaries and was elected deputy for Cordova to the new Cortes in Madrid (December, 1821). Siding with the more radical elements—including Antonio Alcalá Galiano, the literary critic and statesman, with whom he formed a close friendship—he worked as secretary of the Cortes during 1822. At one session in January, 1823, he attracted considerable notice when he made an impassioned speech condemning the attempt by France, Prussia, Australia, and Russia to interfere in the internal affairs of Spain. As Pastor Díaz puts it, he "challenged Europe and the whole world with a bellicose ardor, and his declamations and fiery sentences reached the limits of madness."[4]

During these years (1820–21) the second edition of Saavedra's poems was published. It contained many additions to the poems of 1814, including one of his earliest known compositions, the ballad dated 1806 which begins with the words "On a dapple-gray mare." He also wrote another play, the tragedy *Lanuza*

(1822). This was an eloquent piece of political propaganda, which extolled liberty and condemned despotism; it was performed to thunderous applause in Madrid and in the provinces. But the liberal revolution was to be short-lived: Menacing clouds were forming on the horizon, and the threat of foreign intervention to restore the absolute power of Ferdinand VII became more real with each day. Finally France sent an army into Spain to crush liberalism (1823). Before the threat of the French invasion the Spanish government removed the court to Seville,[5] and the Cortes voted to suspend the king when the latter, on the approach of the French troops, refused to travel to Cádiz. Saavedra voted for the suspension, an act which was to cost him the enmity of Ferdinand. The monarch was finally forced to move from Seville to Cádiz; but the days of the liberals were numbered. Cádiz soon fell to the French, and Ferdinand was free to take his revenge upon the hapless reformists (October, 1823).

III   *Exile*

Saavedra, accompanied by Alcalá Galiano, fled Cádiz on a small boat on October 3. They arrived at Gibraltar on the following day.[6] Don Angel stayed at Gibraltar during the winter and in the following spring embarked on the packet *Francis Freeling* bound for England. He was now an exile in London, stripped of his property and condemned to death by a vengeful Spanish monarch. It was a particularly harsh fate for someone like him, used to the sunny skies of Spain, and especially of Andalusia, a patriot who placed love of Spain above all else in life.

But Saavedra did not let homesickness interfere with his literary production. He wrote two lyric compositions and began work on a narrative poem, *Florinda*, completed two years later. His contacts with other Spanish émigrés in London resulted in the publication in émigré reviews of two poetic compositions he had written during the crossing from Gibraltar to England. Through these contacts, and especially through his friendship with Alcalá Galiano, also in exile in London, he doubtless came to know English poetry and literary criticism of the time. Moreover, as Vicente Lloréns points out, the months Saavedra spent

in London coincide with the development of Romanticism among
the Spanish exiles in the English capital.[7] Thus the young poet
probably was not immune to some of the nascent Romanticism
of émigré literati nor to English Romanticism. The budding
Romanticism seen in the first three cantos of *Florinda*, two of
which were completed in London and a third in Gibraltar after
his departure from England, may very well be due at least
partly to these influences.

The English climate did not agree with Saavedra's health
and he left London at the beginning of January, 1825, with the
idea of making his way to Italy. He stayed six months in Gibraltar; in this time he married Doña María de la Encarnación de
Cueto y Ortega and wrote the third canto of *Florinda*. In the
summer of 1825 he set out with his wife for Italy, but after
arriving at Livorno (Leghorn), he was given to understand by
the Papal authorities and the government of Tuscany, that as a
result of Spanish pressure, he was *persona non grata* in their
states. The Saavedras then left Livorno on a ship bound for
Malta. After a harrowing trip, to which he refers in his famous
poem "El faro de Malta" ("The Lighthouse of Malta"), he
arrived on the Mediterranean island where, due to the pleasant
climate and the friendly welcome he received, he was to stay
for five years writing and painting.

On Malta Saavedra met a man who made a definite impact on
his literary career. He became the friend of John Hookham
Frere, ex-minister plenipotentiary in Madrid, a lover of and
expert in Spanish literature, who resided on the island because of
his wife's poor health. Frere had an extensive library which contained many Spanish works, including an edition of Lope de
Vega's plays and a collection of old Spanish chronicles. According to Pastor Díaz, Frere introduced his young friend to Shakespeare, Byron, and Walter Scott and taught him to appreciate
the "old national Spanish" literature as well as Spanish history
as sources of literary themes.[8] Furthermore, the Englishman
"exhorted him to write with vigor and originality about his own
emotions and his own sensations."[9] Thus, says Pastor Díaz,
Frere caused Saavedra to begin to move away from the Neoclassic style he had cultivated until then and to approach
Romanticism.[10]

Saavedra acknowledged his indebtedness to Frere, both as man and author, in the dedicatory letter, written in English, with which he prefaced *El moro expósito* (*The Foundling Moor*) upon its completion in France. In it he wrote:

You have pointed out, and led me into the path in which I have entered, I am afraid, with more boldness than success. Your friendship has cheered me in the gloomiest days of my exile. Your extensive knowledge and excellent literary taste has made that friendship no less useful than it was pleasing to me. Your love of my dear country has been combined, in my case, with the feelings of concern in my misfortunes and interest for my improvement which I am proud of having excited in you, and the effects of which I have felt and do still feel.[11]

It is difficult to gauge the impact of Frere's friendship on Saavedra's writing. Frere did not really reveal the literary possibilities of Spanish history for Saavedra. After all, *El paso honroso,* which deals with a historical incident, was written as early as 1812; *Florinda,* which treats a semihistorical, semilegendary subject, was begun in London in 1824. As we have seen, the Romantic features of the portion completed before Saavedra met his English mentor may very well reflect his sojourn in England. Furthermore, if we accept Pastor Díaz' assertion and take Saavedra's words to Frere literally, then it certainly took the young man some time to enter the path of Romanticism, for the tragedy *Arias Gonzalo,* written in 1827, is still essentially Neoclassic, and the comedy *Tanto vales cuanto tienes* (*You Are Worth What You Have*; 1828) is also Neoclassic in spirit and in form.[12]

Frere's most important role in his intercourse with the young Spaniard was probably to encourage Saavedra to exploit to the utmost his already existing interest in Spanish history and, in the opinion of Leopoldo Augusto de Cueto, Saavedra's brother-in-law, to make him appreciate the beauty of Spain's old ballads, the *romances.*[13] In this and other respects Frere had doubtless something to do with Saavedra's composition of *El moro expósito,* his long narrative poem whose first five cantos were finished on Malta in 1829. To conclude, it seems reasonable to see in Saavedra's move toward Romanticism a gradual process, beginning to a certain extent in London, perhaps even earlier, which would have ended in a conversion even without Frere, but which Frere hastened somewhat.

Life on Malta was pleasant, and Saavedra was reasonably happy, especially since three children were born to his wife. But he wanted to be nearer Spain, and so in March, 1830, he and his family embarked for France, landing at Marseilles. Pastor Díaz has indicated that the reactionary French government did not allow Saavedra to settle in Paris, forcing him to move to Orléans. This has been repeated by other writers.[14] It seems, however, that Saavedra himself requested permission from the French government to go to Orléans and that permission was granted.[15] In Orléans he opened a school of painting and thus was able to earn a livelihood. After the revolution of July, 1830, Saavedra went to Paris, where he met his friends Istúriz, the ex-president of the Cortes, and Alcalá Galiano, and it was especially with the latter that he renewed an old and close friendship. Pastor Díaz fails to tell us that Saavedra received a financial subsidy from the French government: 200 francs a month in 1831, 150 in 1832, a sum which was later raised to 170 francs and then reduced once more to 150 francs.[16] Thus, while doubtless not living in luxury, he was by no means destitute.

When cholera broke out in Paris in 1832, Saavedra, accompanied by Alcalá Galiano, moved to Tours. His passport, delivered by the French government for the purpose of the journey, described him in the following terms: "Age, 41 years. Height, 1.75 [5'9"]. Hair, black; forehead, regular; eyebrows, light-colored; eyes, grey; nose, large; mouth, medium-sized; beard, brown; chin, round; face, oval-shaped; color, light brown."[17] In Tours Saavedra was able to continue work on *El moro expósito*[18] and to write a version in prose of his great Romantic drama *Don Alvaro o la fuerza del sino* (*Don Alvaro or the Power of Fate*), which was translated into French by Alcalá Galiano, who had hopes—as it happens, unfulfilled—of having the play performed in a Paris theater.

Although his name was not included among those granted amnesty by Ferdinand VII in February, 1833, Saavedra thought it safe enough for his family to return to Spain after he went back to Paris in early 1833. It was in Paris that his *El moro expósito* was published, together with *Florinda,* some lyrics, and historical ballads, in early 1834. *El moro expósito* was very well received in Spain, and the future Duke was now a truly established author.

IV   *The Romantic Years*

In January, 1834, Saavedra was finally able to return to Spain thanks to the extension of the amnesty to thirty-one liberal deputies, including Saavedra, following the death of Ferdinand VII in September, 1833. He had been in exile for more than ten years. This long period was important for his career as a writer. His sojourn in England, on Malta, and in France had acquainted him with the latest literary developments in Western Europe and had doubtless been a factor in his veering toward Romanticism. In 1834, in an article for the English review *The Athenaeum,* Alcalá Galiano, who knew Saavedra well, wrote the following lines on the influence of the exile on his friend's writing:

Saavedra was driven by his mischances to England, and thence to Malta. In the course of his visits to these countries, and of his intercourse with foreign critics, he acquired sounder notions, and more correct information, with respect to the state of European criticism, than most of his fellow-countrymen. His friends who discerned in his conversation indications of a fancy, a wit, and a humour, which were not to be found in his writings, exhorted him to rely fearlessly upon his own powers—to give utterance to that which was within him, instead of repeating that which he had gathered from the works of others.[19]

The frequent mention of fate in Saavedra's work is an indication of the poet's allegiance to Romanticism, but it may also be due partly to some of his experiences during his long exile. At times, as on the perilous voyage from Livorno to Malta, he may very well have come to view himself as the victim of a cruel destiny. The idea of fate, which had always fascinated him—it is found in some of his early poems—, may thus have gathered strength in his mind during those years until it found forceful expression in such works as *El moro expósito* and especially *Don Alvaro*.

On January 9, 1834, Don Angel crossed the Franco-Spanish border at La Junquera. We have an interesting eyewitness account of the future Duke's behavior during the trip by an American naval officer, Alexander Slidell Mackenzie, author of the book *Spain Revisited* (1836), who happened to be one of Saavedra's travel companions. Mackenzie noted the great courtesy with which Saavedra treated servants as well as the affluent persons in the party. He also tells us something of the poet's reaction to his country after ten years of exile:

The face of things seemed to him everywhere improved; and indeed, he was prepared to look on everything with a favouring eye, as he recounted the days of his exile. In England alone he had been hospitably received; in liberal France he found himself scarcely tolerated; watched, annoyed about his passport, and pestered by the police, he had been glad to escape.[20]

In May, 1834, Saavedra's older brother died, and the poet thus inherited the title of duke. As a Spanish grandee he took a seat in the Upper House of the newly established Parliament (July, 1834) and was appointed secretary of that body. On October 9, 1834, the Duke became an honorary member of the Spanish Academy (he was made a regular member in 1846), and on November 26, 1835 he was elected president of the Ateneo of Madrid, the prestigious society for the cultivation of arts and letters. Soon he became vice-president of the Upper House. By this time the Duke had attracted great attention in the literary field. He had put into verse his *Don Alvaro*, making some changes in the process, and had the play produced at the Teatro del Príncipe in Madrid on March 22, 1835. There were eight performances on its first run, a good record for the times if we consider that theatrical runs were generally quite short. The drama also received a good deal of attention in the press and became the subject of a lively controversy. The day of short-lived super-Romanticism in Spain had dawned, and the supporters of the new literary movement applauded the play while Neoclassicists denigrated it.

It was the time of the ferocious first Carlist War (1833–39), fought mostly in the Northeast and East of Spain between the ultraconservative supporters of the Pretender Don Carlos, brother of Ferdinand VII, against the constitutionalist adherents of Queen Isabel II, daughter of Ferdinand, and of her mother, the Regent María Cristina. It was also the time when the liberals split into two camps, the increasingly conservative faction known as *moderados* (moderates) and the more radical *progresistas* (progressives). Rivas, now a grandee and a member of the Upper House, shed his earlier radicalism and joined his friends Alcalá Galiano and Istúriz in opposing the *progresista* government of Mendizábal (1836). After Mendizábal's resignation Rivas was named Minister of the Interior in a *moderado* cabinet. But his exalted position was not to last long. The *progresista* insurrections of August, 1836, caused him to take once more the road to exile, to Portugal and thence to Gibraltar, where he stayed a year and where he wrote some of his historical ballads.

Returning to Spain in August, 1837, he took some part in Spanish politics, but after a few years he went into temporary retirement at Seville, where he lived happily with his family and spent much time on his literary work. The poet José Zorrilla (1817–93), who visited Rivas' house in 1842, has left us a vivid description of the pleasant atmosphere in the Duke's home. He tells us, for instance, how Rivas would read his poetry to his family and friends with great enthusiasm, while his wife and daughters would be working on their needlework and his sons reading or sketching.[21] In 1841, Rivas published his *Romances históricos* (*Historical Ballads*), which must be considered his most valuable contribution to Spanish letters. In those years he also wrote a number of plays, including *El desengaño en un sueño* (*Disillusionment in a Dream*), which was published in 1844, and which next to *Don Alvaro* is his best dramatic work.

V *Spanish Romanticism*

At this point a digression is in order so that we may discuss briefly the nature of Romanticism and its impact on Spanish letters and thus give the reader a clearer idea of the literary atmosphere in which Rivas produced his works. We will try to limit this discussion to its essential aspects.

By the middle of the eighteenth century what has been called a "metaphysical crisis"[22] began to take place in European thought, which was to have a strong impact on literature. Previously established beliefs, especially the belief in the absolute value of reason, suffered a gradual weakening. Sentiment was increasingly stressed, and sentimentality became an accepted way of self-expression. The view of the world as something mechanically and perfectly regulated gave way to the vision of an essentially organic cosmos. Nature in all its aspects, not the regulated nature as can be seen in the gardens of Versailles, but the nature one sees when one travels to the country, began to be intensely appreciated, an attitude caused partly by the writings of Jean-Jacques Rousseau in France.

In literature there developed a growing opposition to Neoclassicism, which had been established definitively in France in the seventeenth century. Neoclassicism emphasized reason, the imitation of nature, the conscious imitation of Greek and Latin models, the didactic function of the literary work, and the application of certain immutable rules purportedly laid down by the Classics of antiquity. What was now beginning to be stressed, however, was feeling, love of nature, and the "sadness of human destiny."[23] This tendency made itself felt with authors like Young (*Night Thoughts*, 1742), Richardson (*Clarissa Harlowe*, 1747), and Gray (*Elegy Written in a Country Churchyard*, 1742–51) in England; Rousseau (*La Nouvelle Héloïse*, 1761) in France; and Goethe (*The Sufferings of Young Werther*, 1774) in Germany. There was also great interest in folk songs and tales of a primitive past. This explains the success of the Scotsman Macpherson's *Poems of Ossian* (1762), which became immensely popular in Continental Europe.

These "pre-Romantics" were followed at the end of the century by full-fledged Romantics who wrote in Germany (Wackenroder, Tieck, and Novalis, guided by the thories of the brothers Schlegel, who incidentally held that the Spanish Baroque drama, and especially Calderón, were highly Romantic), and in England (Wordsworth and Coleridge). Later Arnim, Heine, Uhland in Germany, Byron, Shelley, Keats in England, and Lamartine and Hugo in France, following the precursor Chateaubriand, carried on the torch of Romanticism. The Romantics intensified the tendencies of the pre-Romantics and added new elements. What were some of these elements? The breakdown of the old values and the metaphysical malaise which had been developing in the second half of the eighteenth century led to the Romantic *mal du siècle,* a combination of ennui and anguish which seemed to affect the prominent writers. In their works the Romantic hero—proud, isolated, mysterious, pursued by an irresistible fate, which has been called the "symbol of inability to conciliate earthly experience with belief in a divinely ordained and hence ultimately benevolent, pattern of existence,"[24]—seemed to incarnate this basic disenchantment with the world.

Romanticism proclaimed the value of imagination and the importance of the ego in poetic expression, as well as the importance of passion, and the freedom for the writer to express his passion in whatever way he saw fit. The great Romantic poets in England, Germany, and France sought to "overcome the split between subject and object, the self and the world, the conscious and the unconscious"[25] to a great extent by the use of symbolical imagery in their poetry. The Romantic playwrights stressed the right to mix tragedy and comedy, the sublime and the trivial, and to abolish the Neoclassic unities of time, place, and action, while acknowledging a "unity of interest." Poets, playwrights, and novelists used historical and exotic themes and looked for inspiration in the Middle Ages and the Christian religion.

In Spain Neoclassicism, which received its theoretical foundation with the publication in 1737 of the *Poética* by Ignacio de Luzán, was finally imposed on Spanish letters in the last third of the eighteenth century, after a long struggle, by a relatively small group of intellectuals, backed however by powerful figures in the government. But the reading and theatergoing public never lost interest in the literature of the seventeenth century, especially in the Baroque drama. In Spain, too, sentimentalism and melancholy made their appearance in literature in such figures as the poet Juan Meléndez Valdés (1754–1817), José Cadalso (1741–82), author of the somber *Noches lúgubres* (*Lugubrious Nights*), and the statesman, poet, and playwright Gaspar Melchor de Jovellanos (1744–1811).

But while Romanticism in England and Germany had begun in the last years of the eighteenth century and in France around 1820, the movement took longer to manifest itself in Spain. This was partly due to the devastating war against Napoleon and the despotic regime of Ferdinand VII, who reigned as absolute monarch in 1814–20 and 1823–33, and whose reign inhibited to a certain extent truly innovative literary production, and partly to the considerable influence still wielded by the Neoclassics. Nevertheless, while full-fledged Romanticism came to Spain only after 1833, European Romanticism became known at an earlier date. For instance, Spanish translations of Chateaubriand abounded in the 1820's, and translations of Walter Scott began to circulate in the 1820's, becoming easily accessible between 1830 and 1832. Moreover, between 1814 and 1830 some attempts were made in Spain to popularize Romanticism. A German-born resident of Cádiz, Johann Nikolas Böhl von Faber, translated the portions of the writings of the Schlegel brothers dealing with the Spanish Baroque drama, which they considered essentially Romantic, and sustained, partly in the press, a heated controversy in support of Calderón with the Neoclassic critics José Joaquín de Mora and Antonio Alcalá Galiano (1814–19).

Between 1823 and 1824, a periodical published in Barcelona, *El Europeo,* informed the Spanish public of literary developments abroad and printed some material which can be considered Romantic. The critic and anthologist Agustín Durán (1793–1862) wrote in 1828 a spirited defense of the Baroque drama, claiming that in it may be found the roots of European Romanticism (in the theater, at any rate), and attacking eighteenth-century Neoclassicism.[26] In the same year he began publishing his *Romancero general*, a splendid collection of Spanish ballads, which was preceded by a preface defending the ballad as an artistic genre. Romanticism took another step with the publication of historical novels, drawing on Walter Scott's technique, one of the first being *Los bandos de Castilla o el caballero del cisne (The Factions of Castile or the Knight of the Swan)*, published in 1830 by Ramón López Soler.[27]

It has often been asserted that Spanish Romanticism was brought to Spain by the political émigrés of the 1820's, who became acquainted with it during their exile abroad and introduced it into their native land upon their return in 1833–34. This is somewhat of an exaggeration since Romanticism, as we have seen, was in the air in Spain before this return. On the other hand, it cannot be denied that this exile was an important factor in the spread of Romanticism among Spanish émigrés and hence in Spain after 1833–34. For instance, Romantic verse and prose can be found as early as 1825 in the literary collection entitled *No me olvides* (*Do Not Forget Me*) and published in London by José Joaquín de Mora.[28] We have seen how Saavedra was probably influenced in London by the new literary trends in English literature as well as by those among Spanish exiles and how he was encouraged on Malta to enter new paths which led to *El moro expósito*. The Romantic traits of *Florinda* were probably a result of his sojourn in England, and the controversial *Don Alvaro*, first composed in France, had doubtless some of its roots in the impact made on the young poet by European Romanticism and the success of such Romantic plays as Victor Hugo's *Hernani* (1830) and Alexandre Dumas' *Antony* (1831).

Another political exile, Francisco Martínez de la Rosa (1787–1862), wrote under the influence of French Romanticism a timidly Romantic play in French entitled *Aben-Humeya ou la révolte des Maures sous Philippe II* (*Aben-Humeya or the Revolt of the Moors under Philip II*) and had it performed in Paris in 1830. The poet José de Espronceda (1808–42), who spent some time in England and fought on the barricades in the Paris Revolution of 1830, returned to Spain profoundly influenced by Byron. Alcalá Galiano left Spain a Neoclassic; after his contact with English Romanticism and the Spanish émigré writer José Blanco White, who resided in England, he returned, a mild convert to Romanticism, as his preface to Saavedra's *El moro expósito* shows.[29] Moreover, "the *emigrados* [provided] a powerful impetus to the encouragement of original writers and productions by giving the prestige of their names and initial effort to newer and freer literary forms."[30]

The pace of Romantic growth quickened in 1834. This year saw the publication of Saavedra's *El moro expósito* and of Mariano José de Larra's historical novel *El doncel de Don Enrique el Doliente* (*The Page of Don Enrique the Ailing*

One). It also witnessed the performance in Madrid of Martínez de la Rosa's mildly Romantic *La conjuración de Venecia* (*The Venetian Plot*), as well as that of Larra's *Macías*, a dramatized version of his novel, not yet fully Romantic but nevertheless constituting a strong protest against the despotism of moral law and social convention.

The years 1834–37 were the high point of the Romantic drama, while the early 1840's were the high point of Romantic poetry. *Don Alvaro* (1835) was followed by García Gutiérrez' *El trovador* (*The Troubadour*; 1836), one of the most successful of all Romantic plays, and by Hartzenbusch's *Los amantes de Teruel* (*The Lovers of Teruel*; 1837), another highly charged Romantic drama. They were also the years when the influence of Victor Hugo and Alexandre Dumas was strongest in Spain. Between 1835 and 1838 Hugo's plays were "translated and performed continually, not only in Madrid, but in the provinces."[31] Dumas was more popular even than Victor Hugo and had a strong influence on a number of Spanish writers.[32] As for poetry, the early 1840's saw the publication of Espronceda's lyric poems, of his highly Romantic *El diablo mundo* (*The Diabolical World*), of Rivas' magnificent *Romances históricos* (*Historical Ballads*), and of José Zorrilla's *Cantos del trovador* (*Songs of the Troubadour*).

In the writings of the Romantics of those years we find a number of ingredients that shape European Romanticism: melancholy, the exaltation of love, exotic themes and others drawn from national history, picturesqueness, local color, the horrible and the grotesque, and in the theater a disregard of the unities, the mixture of comedy and tragedy, melodramatic scenes and violent contrasts. Some of the more metaphysical aspects of European Romanticism also found an echo, though not a strong one, among the Spanish Romantics. The *mal du siècle,* the deep pessimism, the subjectivity, the new interpretation of the world and society, the characters who revolt against the cosmos and society can be seen, though not always convincingly, in the poems of Espronceda, the most subjective and Byronic of all Spanish Romantics; in some of the writings of the great satirist Mariano José de Larra (1809–37), who committed suicide at the age of twenty-eight, perhaps the most Romantic of them all if we consider his deeply pessimistic view of the world and of Spanish society; in the poems of a few secondary figures, such as Pastor Díaz, and to a certain extent in Rivas' *Don Alvaro* and in a few other Romantic plays.[33]

These manifestations of what we might call extreme Romanticism provoked a strong defense of traditional Catholic values[34] and reinforced within the movement something which had been present in it since its inception, a tendency to draw its themes from Spanish history and to be satisfied with the more external trappings of Romanticism. Because of the "impossibility that the new ideas, the new interpetation of the world, the new revolutionary and unorthodox philosophy of Romanticism, could take root in the orthodox and Catholic soil of Spain,"[35] Spanish Romanticism, after some manifestations of "rebellion" on the European model (mostly during the period 1835–40), became ever more "nationalized" and moderate. In the drama and in narrative poetry, especially, it intensified the integration of the more external Romantic ingredients—such as Romantic picturesqueness, sentimentality, and rhetoric—with traditional themes, often derived from Spanish history and legend, and eliminated in the process the exaggerations and the "immoral" elements which were denounced by some contemporary critics as shocking. Examples of this nationalization are the historical drama *Guzmán el Bueno* (*Guzmán the Great*; 1842) by Gil y Zárate; the immensely popular *Don Juan Tenorio* (1844) by Zorrilla, a play which, though dealing with the Don Juan figure, treats a traditionally Spanish theme and ends on a deeply religious note; the *leyendas* (legends) of Zorrilla, and the *leyendas* of Rivas (begun in 1847), which emphasize religion and nationalism.

It must also be kept in mind that Romantic plays, even at the height of the Romantic "revolt" (1834–37),[36] did not monopolize the stage. "All that is true is that the number of Romantic plays in the repertory of the Madrid theaters from 1834 onward increased for relatively few years, but they never constituted a majority of the theatrical offerings."[37] This is also probably true for other Spanish cities. Although Romanticism could still produce in the 1860's the intensely lyric poetry and the legends in prose of that greatest of nineteenth-century poets, Gustavo

Adolfo Bécquer (1836–70), its force was essentially spent by the middle of the century.[38]

VI *Rivas in the Service of His Country*

In 1844, the Duke, who had become quite conservative, was named Spanish minister plenipotentiary—a title later changed to ambassador—to the Kingdom of Naples and Sicily. While the first impressions made upon him by his new environment were negative, he soon came to like Naples and its beautiful surroundings. Making the acquaintance of outstanding Neapolitan men of letters, he was to divide his time between his diplomatic duties and his literary interests. On April 28, 1845, he wrote to the conservative General Narváez, who was then in charge of the Spanish government: "I am happy every day here, I am respected and esteemed and I am in perfect health."[39]

In Naples Rivas wrote some lyric poems, two prose sketches about excursions to surrounding areas, the *Sublevación de Nápoles, capitaneada por Masaniello* (*The Revolt of Naples Led by Masaniello*; 1847), dealing with the Neapolitan uprising against Spanish rule in 1647, and *La azucena milagrosa* (*The Miraculous Lily*), the first of the three legends which were to be his last important poetic work. Recalled in July, 1850 over some diplomatic differences that had arisen between the Spanish and Neapolitan governments, Rivas settled in Madrid and began to write again, though politics would once more make demands upon him in the following years. Products of this period are the legends *Maldonado* and *El aniversario* (*The Anniversary*), which appeared in the collected edition of 1854–55. This edition contained only the works which the Duke himself considered suitable for publication, omitting almost all of his Neoclassic plays. In June, 1857, he was appointed Ambassador to France. His short stay in Paris was on the whole a happy one. He was on intimate terms with many noble French families and, more important, with Emperor Napoleon III and the Empress Eugénie. The fact that the latter was Spanish made his relations with the French court particularly pleasant. On August 14, 1857, Rivas wrote to Narváez: "I went at one o'clock, in formal dress. The Emperor received me by shaking my hand and speaking to me with the greatest deference and left me in the cabinet of the Empress, alone with her, where I remained 'tête à tête' [with her] until a quarter to three."[40]

VII *The Last Years*

Shortly after his return to Spain from Paris in July, 1858, Rivas was struck by an incurable disease which was to take him to his grave. He bore his illness with great courage but was nonetheless distressed that he was no longer able to write. Yet he could be seen attending conferences and lectures leaning on a friend and still gaining by his charm the sympathy of all those who had dealings with him.

The almost constant pain which he had to endure prevented him from completing a ballad on the Spanish-Moroccan War of 1859–60, which was to be included in a collection entitled *Romancero de la guerra de Africa* (*Collection of Ballads on the African War*), and the final version of this poem, entitled *Indignación de España* (*Indignation of Spain*) is the joint work of the Marquis of Molins and himself.

More honors were to be awarded him in his final years. He was elected Director of the Spanish Academy upon the death of Martínez de la Rosa in 1862, and in 1863 he was appointed President of the Council of State. When he retired from this position in 1864, he was decorated by Queen Isabel II with the Collar of the Golden Fleece. He died on June 22, 1865. Intellectual Spain felt the loss keenly. There was a "sense of complete prostration, of irreparable personal loss,"[41] for Spanish writers and the reading public realized that an outstanding member of their literary community had passed away.

CHAPTER 2

Saavedra's Neoclassic Period: Early Poetry and Drama

I Early Lyrics

IN his youth Saavedra was strongly influenced by the Neo-classic trends which dominated Spanish literature from the last third of the eighteenth century to the early 1830's. The rules evolved by Aristotle, Horace, and Longinus and their modern commentators were his guides. The imitation and praise of an idealized nature, verisimilitude, and clarity of expression were some of the things he sought to achieve in his poetry. Since eighteenth-century Spanish Neoclassic poets considered that the simplicity and clarity of the Greek and Latin Classics had been most successfully imitated by Spain's sixteenth-century poets such as Garcilaso de la Vega, Fernando de Herrera, and Luis de León, they endeavored to emulate these writers. Poets such as Diego Tadeo González and Juan Meléndez Valdés (1754–1817) and many others poured forth a steady stream of relatively Classic simplicity in the form of ballads, odes, sonnets, and various other verse forms, frequently bucolic and addressed to certain allegedly beloved shepherdesses, likely to have Arcadian names such as Delia, Mirta, Melisa, Filis, Lisi, etc.

In a foreword to the 1814 edition of his poems, Saavedra speaks of having tried to imitate the simplicity of expression of Spain's sixteenth-century poets. Many of the first poems of the future Duke are light, graceful enough, metrically correct, smooth in expression, but of no deep inspiration. He called many of the ladies to whom he addressed his early poems by such names as Flora, Filena, Celinda, Amira, Lesbia, and, for a group of later poems, Olimpia. In addition to the names employed, there are numerous Classical and mythological refer-

32

ences: Phoebus (or Phoebus' chariot), Venus, Flora, Favonius, and Alcides figure prominently.

Yet his first known composition, a *romance* or ballad dated 1806, goes back to the Middle Ages for its subject; it has considerable color and a glamorized gallant and enamored Moorish hero. In other words we have a first faint anticipation of Romanticism, pointing toward Saavedra's longest poem, *The Foundling Moor* (1834). The main distinction of this early poem is its preoccupation with horses. How Saavedra loved horses! We observe here, as in many subsequent cases, that the color of the horse is given, as well as its sex. The poem begins: "En una yegua tordilla," that is, "On a dapple-gray mare." It would not really matter to most readers on what kind of horse the noble Moor Atarfe was riding, but Saavedra wished to identify it.

The Napoleonic invasion of 1808–14 inspired numerous poets, notably Quintana, to compose patriotic odes, and Saavedra contributed his share. His first one was signed "In a military camp, 1808," and is entitled *To the Arming of the Spanish Provinces Against the French.* Further patriotic poems celebrate the victories of Bailén and Arapiles, the dethronement of Napoleon, and the final victory of Spanish arms. These compositions, like other patriotic pieces of the era, are emphatic and high-sounding, with resonant phrases and grandiose statements. The ultimate source of all such poems is the great sixteenth-century poet Fernando de Herrera.

Saavedra was a compulsive poetizer, and military campaigns and even serious wounds did not stop his urge. Even when he was in a hospital in 1809, after being left for dead on the battlefield at Ontígola, he wrote a ballad in eleven quatrains to his nurse, whom he calls Filena, and who has never been identified. It is the composition, well-known to all admirers of Saavedra, which begins—and we imitate the rhythm of the original:

> With eleven mortal wounds,
> With my sword dashed into fragments,
> And my horse no longer breathing,
> And the battle gone against us . . .[1]

By far the most interesting group of lyrics of Saavedra to appear before his exile are those addressed to a lady whom he calls Olimpia, who has already been mentioned. She has never been publicly identified, though Saavedra's friends must have known perfectly well who she was. They belong to the years 1819–20 and must definitely refer to some real passion of the future Duke, twenty-eight years old at that time. The tone is different from the little trifles addressed to other ladies who are given Classical or pastoral names, and it is much easier to believe that the poet meant much of what he was saying in various verse forms. There is a feeling of almost Romantic despair in the following lines:

> Oh terrible woman! . . . And what has become
> Of your promises, your treacherous tears?
> What power has broken our bonds?
>
> .   .   .   .
>
> Oh, the happy days are gone
> When longingly, fired with passion, mad with love,
> You promised me matchless constancy. (p. 60)

The compositions of Saavedra's years of exile show contradictory characteristics. On the one hand the personal note becomes more accented, and melancholy is quite marked. But on the other, there are many Classical allusions, and conventional phrases still weigh down his poems. *El desterrado* (*The Banished Man*) is a rather long, personal, and moving composition, written on shipboard in May of 1824, as the future Duke was leaving Gibraltar. It contains the natural laments of a man who feels that he had patriotically served and fought for his beloved country and now finds himself rejected, thrown into undeserved exile. No wonder he exclaims: "Oh fatherland! Ungrateful fatherland! . . . Thou dost drive me / With frightful fury from thy bosom, / Rewarding thus my love!" (p. 497). Probably remembering the words of Aeneas "Fuit Troya," he says "España fue," meaning that Spain no longer is (p. 497). In the last two quatrains he hopes that his fatherland will be avenged and that the day may come when he will see "Fair Hesperia" free, triumphant, and glorious, so that he will die happy. When the author later collected his compositions for an edition of his works, he eliminated the following lines which by then he considered too anti-monarchical: "Let the cowardly heart of the stupid king / Burn with renewed fury, / The king who was blindly adored / By barbarians, and let this iniquitous man / Display his perfidy with new cruelty."[2] In form most of the lines are the conventional hendecasyllables, but heptasyllables are also used, including four quatrains which are entirely heptasyllabic.

Three years after Saavedra had reached his island refuge he wrote a poem which has consistently been acclaimed as one of his best, marking his real conversion to Romanticism. It is entitled "El faro de Malta" ("The Lighthouse of Malta"). The twenty unrhymed stanzas were obviously not the result of sudden inspiration, since they were composed long after Saavedra's actual arrival. There are still Neoclassic elements observable in the short composition: conventional phrases, like those previously used by the author, such as "hoarse hurricane," "white foam," "stormy clouds," "gentle night," and the use of Latium as a name for Italy. Yet this poem evidently marks something new, not only in its non-Classic form, but in its spirit. It is more subjective, more emotional, more nostalgic, and more suggestive. The light itself symbolizes safety and peace after passage through the treacherous reefs and shoals of life. It is also "Like the torch of reason / In the midst of the fury of the passions / Or of the sly blandishments of fortune" (p. 503). To the Saavedra couple, as to many other "poor, persecuted refugees," this lighthouse meant refuge and hospitality. The last stanzas, especially the final two, are the most personal of all. The poet loves and cherishes Malta, but he would exchange its beneficent light "For the flame and the refulgent gleams / Which shine forth as the rising sun strikes / The golden Archangel [the statue of the patron of the city] which crowns / Cordova's tower" (p. 504). This is what Alcalá Galiano had to say about the poem:

His lines to the Beacon Light of Malta are very spirited, and their author in them gave a specimen of the new poetical principles which he had adopted. The idea of mentioning the weather-vane (in the form of a gilded angel) which crowns the steeple of the cathedral of Cordoba, would probably have been rejected by most of the living authors of Spain, as an image unbefitting poetry of a high order; and yet it is good, because natural, and well concludes his fanciful and affecting poem.[3]

II *Early Narrative Poems*

The first long poem by the future Duke in four cantos and a total of 243 royal octaves, i.e., eight-line stanzas of hendecasyllables rhyming *abababcc*, was included in his first published volume of poetry (1814). It is entitled *El paso honroso*, which we might translate as *The Passage at Arms* and paraphrase as *The Honorable Keeping of the Bridge*, and was composed in Cádiz in 1812. The hero of this poem, which could be called a romance of chivalry, is Don Suero de Quiñones, an ancestor of Saavedra, whose historical deeds the author decides to utilize. Suero de Quiñones, a courtier of King John II (1407–54), was a man in love, so much so that he made a vow to wear an iron collar or ring around his neck until his lady relented and granted him her favor. The situation, and probably the collar, became uncomfortable, and Don Suero sought honorable means to get out of both. On Friday, January 1, 1434, he and nine chosen companions, during festivities at Medina del Campo, requested King John to allow them to defend a bridge at San Marcos de Orbigo, between Astorga and León, for a month, against all comers. The King authorized the affair, and challenges were widely distributed; sixty-eight knights, in fact, accepted, including some non-Spaniards. The arrangements took more than six months, but the combats actually began on July 10, 1434 and lasted until August 19. The judges overseeing the combats professed themselves satisfied by Suero's and his men's performances. Don Suero took off the iron ring which had confined his neck, and his lady gave him her hand.

The proceedings were recorded by an eyewitness whose report was published more than a century later in Salamanca by a Franciscan friar, Juan de Pineda.[4] The book must surely have been in the Rivas library, and young Angel de Saavedra must have read it and accepted it as absolute fact. But the chronicle of Pineda was by no means the only source of his

poem. The author obviously had in mind Ariosto, Tasso, and
Pedro de Espinosa (1578–1650), author of a poem called *Fable
of the Genil* (the Genil is a little river which flows into the
Guadalquivir), noted anthologist and prose writer. Naturally
Saavedra pays general tribute to Homer and Virgil and takes
suggestions from eighteenth-century poets such as Diego Tadeo
González and Nicolás Fernández de Moratín.[5]

The poetic form and the style are conventional enough, following the epics of Ariosto and Tasso and their Spanish imitators
of the sixteenth and seventeenth centuries.[6] The first three
stanzas are unimpressive invocations. Stanza 3 is addressed to
". . . divine Lesbia, whom my heart adores, / Sighing for you . . ."
(p. 69), and so on. Saavedra had also addressed a sonnet to
Lesbia, apparently at the same period, but her identity is
unknown, and judging by the rest of the poem she does not
matter at all. Despite all these conventionalities and the generally Neoclassic tone, we would normally consider the events
and the setting of the poem as highly Romantic. Saavedra, following the dry facts furnished by Pineda, did his best to
make the account as picturesque as possible and to give the
poem color and vigor. Unfortunately there is a monotony in
the narrative pattern—warrior after warrior is described in turn—
which is not offset by many felicitous passages, and the abundance of Classical allusions is wearisome. The poem comes to
a rather abrupt conclusion with the following lines:

> And at the sound of trumpets and drums,
> Without the ring, he kneels before his lady,
> Who says to him, her face suffused with blushes:
> Noble Quiñones, rise, you are my husband. (p. 94)

More ambitious than *El paso honroso* is Saavedra's narrative
poem *Florinda*, which was composed between 1824 and 1826,[7]
but which appeared in Paris in 1834, together with *El moro
expósito*. A semi-epic poem, written in royal octaves like *El
paso honroso*, it deals with the legend of Rodrigo, the last of
the Visigothic kings, and the "Loss of Spain." According to this
traditional legend, King Rodrigo, from his palace in Toledo,
looked down and saw the beautiful Florinda, also called La

Cava, at her bath. Smitten with love, he gained possession of her. Her father, Count Julián, Governor of Ceuta, was enraged, and sought vengeance with the aid of Don Oppas, Bishop of Seville, by bringing African troops over to destroy Rodrigo. Their mission was accomplished with the Moslem victory over the Goths on the banks of the Guadalete in 711 A.D.

Saavedra, like all Spaniards and many foreigners, of course knew the legend and no doubt many variants. Obviously he knew enough to compose a poem on the subject without consulting any books at all. There are, however, several with which he may have been familiar. According to the great Spanish scholar Ramón Menéndez Pidal, *Florinda* was written on the basis of two late eighteenth-century works, one a tragedy called *Florinda*, by one of the aspiring and not too well-known dramatists of the epoch, Rosa Gálvez, and the other a "historical novel" called *Rodrigo* (1793), by the rather fertile ex-Jesuit Pedro Montengón. The hypothesis is possible, though there are no convincing proofs. Menéndez Pidal further thinks that the conception of *Florinda* was at least modified by Byron's tragedy *Sardanapalus*, which had been published in 1821 and was obviously available.[8] It is perfectly true that the Myrrha of Byron's work was what we would now call a sort of party-girl, keen on banquets and festivities, as is Florinda, but there are really few other similarities. There are three other works in English whose possible influence Menéndez Pidal discards, but their influence is still possible. One is Walter Scott's *The Vision of Don Roderick* (1811). Another is Walter Savage Landor's *Count Julian* (1812), a closet drama now thoroughly forgotten. Still another is Robert Southey's wordy *Roderick*, published in 1814, the year after Southey became poet laureate.

It is easy to point out the chief faults of *Florinda*. The characterization is seriously lacking in sharpness, and the style is overblown. The modern reader is likely to tire of the succession of highly rhetorical lines and of the superfluity of mythological references, which seem even to increase in the last two cantos. Some are mere clichés; the god Mars is particularly overworked. Yet the poem does not deserve the poor esteem in which the author himself and some critics held it.[9] Many of the scenes are imaginatively presented and picturesque, and the descriptions are an integral part of the structure. There are considerably more passages of real lyric attractiveness than in *El paso honroso,* over which *Florinda* marks an important advance. Saavedra was not precocious, and he reached real artistic maturity rather slowly, but in his thirties he writes with a definitely surer touch.

In spite of the Classical form of *Florinda* and the use of mythological references, the poem definitely shows an approach to Romantic procedures. Allison Peers has pointed out certain features: The subject is medieval and national, and the passion of the principal characters is emphasized, because Florinda and Rodrigo are by no means bound by any ideas of Classic restraint. There is an obvious seeking for picturesqueness, and even an emphasis on scenes of horror, on mystery.[10] The necromancer Rubén is no Classic figure, even though he is not carefully characterized. The Jewish physician or magician became an almost obligatory figure in typically Romantic productions. The description of his mysterious castle in *Florinda* suggests that Saavedra had probably read Walpole or Anne Radcliffe or Monk Lewis, although proof is lacking.

In Saavedra's previous works one can note references to fate, but by no means as many as in *Florinda.* In stanza XIV of Canto I we learn that Rubén can read the fate of the living from the stars. At the banquet his powers enable him to predict the dreadful fate of those present. In stanza XLIV Count Julián speaks of his "dreadful destiny" and repeats the idea three stanzas later. The idea of fate broods over the whole composition. The author also shows a greater sensitivity to light and shade, even to color. All in all, *Florinda* marks a considerable advance in the poet's art. Peers summarizes by quoting a friend of Saavedra, the critic Manuel Cañete, who said: "The aforesaid work is the point at which the former principles which were the poet's standard begin to fuse or combine with the new doctrines destined to regenerate it."[11]

III *Plays*

Between 1814 and 1828 Saavedra wrote seven Neoclassic tragedies and one comedy .In these plays he did his best to follow the precepts handed down by the Italian and French commentators of Aristotle and Horace, assigning men of high estate and their passions to the tragedies, dealing with the behavior of common men and their amusing foibles in the comedy, and observing the unities of action, time, and place.

The first of the tragedies, *Ataúlfo*, written in 1814, was not played or printed, as it was prohibited by the public censor, and the manuscript of the second, *Doña Blanca* (1815), was lost in the turmoils of 1823. The third tragedy, *Aliatar* (1816), was performed successfully in Seville, in July, 1816. Although Neoclassic in form, this play takes place in the Middle Ages, during the late stages of the Christian Reconquest of Spain, and deals with the love of a Moorish chieftain, Aliatar, for his Christian captive Elvira. Moreover, it ends in the suicide of the protagonist after he stabs Elvira. Thus, potentially Romantic elements are present. The struggle in the soul of Aliatar, enslaved by an uncontrollable passion for the Christian Elvira, is well-developed, and the deaths of the Moslem chieftain and his Christian slave seem to be the logical and inevitable outcome of the love of Aliatar for Elvira. The meter, the assonant hendecasyllable line, is the one used by Saavedra throughout his tragedies, and it makes the action sound prosaic at times. Yet the tragic tension is successfully maintained throughout. *Aliatar* is in some respects the play of a novice, but it is fairly elegantly carried off.

Saavedra's next two plays were performed in various parts of Spain including Seville.[12] The first, *El Duque de Aquitania* (*The Duke of Aquitania*; 1817), written like his other tragedies in five acts, is a weak imitation of *Oreste* by the Italian playwright Alfieri. The second, *Malek-Adhél* (1818), is of greater merit. Based on a long novel by Madame Cottin entitled *Mathilde* and published in London in French in 1805, it presents the tragic love of Malek-Adhél, brother of the Sultan Saladin, and Mathilde, sister of the English king Richard the Lion Hearted, in Palestine at the time of the Crusades. The conflict in the souls of these two protagonists is developed in a lofty tone appropriate to their high stations in life. Although Nicholson B. Adams feels that Saavedra "failed to absorb characteristics of an early Romanticism" from Madame Cottin,[13] it is of some interest to note that the last act has some Romantic aspects. There is a somber atmosphere worthy of a play by Victor Hugo or Alexandre Dumas as the action takes place in a sepulchral chapel at the tomb of the French crusader, Montmorency. There is a desperate quality in the behavior of Malek-Adhél, who beseeches Mathilde to follow him. Then, toward the end, when the arrogant and intolerant Lusiñán tries to seize Mathilde, Malek-Adhél endeavors to defend the girl, and the action explodes into violence as the hateful Lusiñán has his men murder his rival. Indeed, a scene which might adorn a Romantic play!

The tragedy *Lanuza* is mainly a piece of liberal propaganda, the product of Saavedra the liberal, supporting the cause of liberalism with his pen in 1822. Saavedra in this play is obviously addressing his countrymen and urging them to fight for the triumph of liberty in their land. The story is that of the young chief justice of Aragón, Lanuza, who, revolting against the absolutism of King Philip II in 1591, is abandoned by most of his followers, made a prisoner by the troops of the King, and beheaded. The play is full of references to liberty and to the struggle to preserve it, something that must have made it most attractive to the liberal public of 1823, when it was performed to thunderous applause. Lanuza's last words have the ring of a political harangue: "A day will come, I foresee it, / When reason and justice will triumph, / When the virtuous will conquer evil, / And when the whole world will enjoy freedom, / Once the chains of opprobrium are broken.... / And glorious Spain shall be the first / To utter the cry that will save the universe."[14]

The setting of Saavedra's last tragedy, *Arias Gonzalo* (1827),[15] the siege of Zamora by King Sancho of Castile in the eleventh century, had been treated in many old Spanish ballads as well as in the medieval *First General Chronicle*[16] and in plays by Juan de la Cueva (1550?–1610?), Lope de Vega (1562–1635), and Guillén de Castro (1569–1631). The play follows a very simple line. After King Sancho is murdered by the Zamoran Bellido Dolfos not far from the Castilian encampment, the Castilian knight Diego Ordóñez de Lara challenges the city of Zamora; the challenge is accepted by Arias Gonzalo, tutor and counselor of the Infanta Doña Urraca, lady of Zamora. His three sons will fight Ordóñez. The youngest son of Arias Gonzalo, Gonzalo Arias, is in love with Urraca and she returns his love. He finally kills Ordóñez after his two brothers are slain by the Castilian, but he himself is mortally wounded. The play ends with Urraca fainting from grief and Arias Gonzalo exclaiming: "Zamora is free, / But alas, how much this costs Arias Gonzalo" (p. 152).

Here, where Saavedra deals with a traditional Spanish theme, he succeeds in imparting more life to the tragedy than in his previous attempts in the drama, with the exception perhaps of *Lanuza*. He captures the epic flavor of the clash between the Leonese of Zamora and the Castilians represented by Diego Ordóñez de Lara. The latter issues his *reto* or challenge in a forceful language reminiscent of the old ballads dealing with the siege: "I accuse you, Infanta, the magnates, / The knights, squires and the populace / Of this wicked town; the young men, / And the children, and the old men, and the women; / Those who have not been born yet and the remains / Which sleep in the dishonored tombs, / Of being treacherous, infamous, and perfidious" (p. 141).

The love of Gonzalo Arias for Urraca is subordinated to the epic theme of the resistance of Zamora to the Castilians. But the few indications of a budding Romanticism, aside from the fact that the play deals with a national and medieval subject, are found precisely in this lyrical aspect of *Arias Gonzalo*. The play would be even more attractive—and this can be said of all of Saavedra's tragedies—if the action had not been rigidly encased within the twenty-four-hour limit prescribed by Neoclassic dramatic theory. The action takes place between the middle of the morning and nightfall, and the element of verisimilitude suffers as reader and spectator must accept the fact that the death of the king of Castile, the challenge of Ordóñez, and the death of the three brothers, as well as the declaration of love of Gonzalo to Urraca can happen in so short a span of time.

In 1828, while still on Malta, Saavedra found time to write a light comedy in three acts, *Tanto vales cuanto tienes* (*You Are Worth What You Have*). A comedy of manners in verse (although letters are read in prose), it follows in the footsteps of the foremost Spanish Neoclassic playwright Leandro Fernández de Moratín (1760–1828), whose comedies were written according to the Neoclassic precepts of the observance of the three unities of action, time, and place, and of the importance of the moral message. It also has something of the spirit of the playwright Bretón de los Herreros (1796–1873), who started by imitating Moratín and went on to perfect his own brand of comedy of manners.[17] The place is a sitting room and the time lapse is well within twenty-four hours—this can be gathered only through internal evidence because the author does not indicate it explicitly at the beginning of the play.

A rich bachelor, Don Blas, returns from America, wishing to bestow his wealth on his brother and sister, whom he had already aided. To test them, he pretends to have lost his fortune at sea, and all except his niece, Doña Paquita, scorn him. His sister, Doña Rufina, practically kicks him out of her house, for to her wealth is the only value. She has borrowed heavily from a usurer, Don Simeón, to impress her brother. When the latter reveals that his wealth is intact, she does the expected amount of teeth-gnashing. So the sweet niece and her fiancé are rewarded.

The message of the play is clear enough. The servant Ana, who sees through her mistress Doña Rufina, says at one point: "In the ups and downs of the world, / Since interest reigns supreme, / There is only one rule, which is: / You are worth what you have" (p. 269). Thus the author condemns greed—incarnated by Rufina, her brother Alberto, and her cousin Miguel —and extols virtue—personified by Don Blas and Doña Paquita. There is a scene between these two characters that has all the earmarks of a passage from a *comédie larmoyante*, the "tearful," sentimental comedy so much in vogue in the eighteenth century and whose impact is also found in Moratín's masterpiece *El sí de las niñas (Girls' Consent*; 1806). When Paquita, thinking that Don Blas is now a poor man, offers to her uncle a pearl necklace which he had once sent her as a present, Don Blas cannot hold back his tears, and we are reminded of some scenes in *El sí de las niñas* which overflow with sentimentality.

Much of the comic effect in this amiable and not unattractive play is due to the behavior of Doña Rufina. There is no attempt on the part of the author to create in her a complex character. She is essentially a caricature, the incarnation of greed and arrogance, who behaves ignobly not only toward her brother Blas but also toward her own daughter, and who justly receives not a penny of Blas' fortune. Her behavior borders frequently upon the farcical. Her comic disappointment and her arrogance are shown in her angry outburst at her brother when she finds out that he has allegedly lost all his money: "You big bore . . . ! / Have you ever seen such a fool? / So, you big blockhead, / This is the way you lost all our money?" (p. 266).

Another comic character is the old money lender Don Simeón. He, too, is a caricature in his outrageous greed which causes him to lend money to Rufina and her relatives at the rate of 100% interest. Don Simeón, who is on stage for a good part of the first act and appears also in Acts II and III, forms a striking contrast with the virtuous Don Blas who with Paquita represents the positive element of society. Together with Rufina, Alberto, and Miguel, Don Simeón symbolizes the greed and corruption that prevail in much of the world and which Saavedra condemns so heartily in this play.

CHAPTER 3

Saavedra's Emancipation from Neoclassicism: El moro expósito

I *Alcalá Galiano's Preface*

SAAVEDRA'S decisive break with Neoclassicism came with the writing of the long poem entitled *El moro expósito* (*The Foundling Moor*). Begun in Malta it was finished in Paris in 1833 and published there in 1834. The dedication to John Hookham Frere[1] was followed by a preface. Since it is unsigned, readers must have presumed that it was by Saavedra. Not so, however; the 1854 edition puts matters right: "Prólogo de la edición de París escrito a nombre del autor por el Excmo. Señor D. Antonio Alcalá Galiano" (Preface of the Paris Edition Written in the Name of the Author by the Distinguished Don Antonio Alcalá Galiano"). This now famous preface is regarded as the most important manifesto of Romanticism in Spain and has been compared to the *Préface du 'Cromwell'* (1827) of Victor Hugo. It is not so violent or revolutionary as we might expect. Alcalá Galiano begins by speaking of the opposing sects of Romantics and Classicists. He attributes the birth of the new movement to Germany and rapidly comments on French, English, Italian, and Spanish literature, insisting that literature must be representative of its own country and time. Here is a significant statement:

. . . the rule must always be observed that only that is poetic and good which declares the flights of fancy and the emotions of the spirit. Everything that is vague, indefinable, inexplicable in the mind of man; everything that moves us, either by arousing surprise or tenderness; whatever depicts characters in which we see the ideal coupled with the natural, creations in short which are not copies, but whose identity with real and true objects we feel, know,

45

and confess; in fine, all that arouses in us recollections of strong emotions; good and genuine poetry is all that and nothing else.[2]

Alcalá Galiano then goes on to say that a new doctrine in various nations "has broken the chain of respected traditions, and given a mortal blow to certain authorities considered infallible up to the present" (p. xxix). He then speaks of the "metaphysical" poetry of Byron, Coleridge, Wordsworth, Hugo, and Lamartine. Of *El moro expósito* he says that the author has not sought to make it either Classic or Romantic, "arbitrary divisions in which he does not believe," and goes on to state that he has chosen a subject from the history of Spain and of the Middle Ages; he has adopted a verse scheme rarely or never used in long works, capable of elegance and pomp, which is, with its assonance, true Spanish poetry; but he has avoided an even and sustained style and any allusions to Classical mythology. He has written passages of an elevated style as well as others expressed in plain language, and his language is often prosaic and humble. He has sought to give his composition the proper color. He has not blindly followed anyone's style, not even that of Fernando de Herrera, whom he much admired. In short, the poem does not observe "certain rules which have repeatedly been condemned by learned critics and which are not followed by the best contemporary poets in Europe. . . . [It] is licit to affirm that [the author] has pointed out a path not trodden by his compatriots" (pp. xxxiii–xxxiv).

While this preface is not particularly revolutionary and Alcalá Galiano is careful to say that the author does not believe in the Classic-Romantic polarization, we should keep in mind that he nevertheless emphasizes that this work must be considered a new departure in Spanish literature. This, together with Saavedra's statement in his dedication to Frere concerning the "path in which I have entered," proves that Saavedra, while writing the poem, had been perfectly aware of the fact that he had at least tilted strongly toward Romanticism. The extent of this tilt will be discussed later in this chapter.

II *The Legend of the Seven Infantes of Lara*

As Alcalá Galiano states, the subject of *El moro expósito* is taken from the Middle Ages. The work, whose subtitle is

Córdoba y Burgos en el siglo décimo (*Cordova and Burgos in the Tenth Century*), is based on a medieval Castilian tradition. That there is a historical basis for this tradition is possible, but we do not know with any certainty what historic deed inspired the tale. Thus, all that can be said is that *El moro expósito* is based on a legend, the legend of *los siete infantes de Lara* (the seven noble-born sons of Lara), which captivated the imagination of countless Spaniards throughout the ages and was celebrated in many literary works. Chronologically, our first contact with it is through the thirteenth-century *Crónica General* (*General History*), written at the order of Alfonso X of Castile, in which an old epic poem dealing with the seven infantes is preserved in the form of historical prose. The content of this lost *cantar de gesta* (epic poem) is briefly as follows:

The Castilian knight Rui-Velázquez, prodded by the complaints of his wife Doña Lambra, who had been gravely offended by his nephews, the seven young *infantes* of the house of Lara, betrays the latter to the Moors. They are captured and beheaded, and their heads are taken to Cordova where they are seen by their father Gonzalo Gustios, who is held prisoner by the Moorish prime minister Almanzor. But Almanzor's sister falls in love with Gonzalo, and some time after Gonzalo is freed and returns to Castile, she gives birth to a child whose name will be Mudarra. Eventually Mudarra goes to Castile and avenges his brothers by killing Rui-Velázquez and having Doña Lambra burned alive.[3]

III *The Plot*

Saavedra's poem is written mostly in hendecasyllabic quatrains with assonance in the even-numbered lines[4] and is divided into twelve cantos which the author calls *romances*. It is a long poem which runs to more than 14,000 lines, accompanied by introductions and notes.

At the beginning of *El moro expósito*, we learn of the death of Zahira, sister of Almanzor, the premier to the Caliph of Cordova. Zahira had brought up a young foundling, whose education she had entrusted to the great Zaide. The foundling, whose name is Mudarra, has reached the age of nineteen. He is passion-

ately in love with the beautiful and virtuous Kerima, daughter
of the former prime minister Giafar. The festivities which take
place on the occasion of the marriage of Almanzor's son see the
young foundling perform superbly in the lists and receive the
prize from Kerima at Almanzor's orders, to the chagrin of Giafar,
her father. The latter has been planning to marry his daughter
to another man and decides to do away with Mudarra. He lures
the young foundling into an ambush, but Mudarra kills him.
Zaide, to whom Mudarra tells what he has done, relates to his
friend the circumstances of his birth. He is the son of Zahira
and of the Castilian knight Gonzalo Gustios de Lara, who had
once vanquished Zaide in combat (although he had treated him
with great courtesy). Lara, sent on a dangerous mission to
Cordova by his villainous brother-in-law Rui-Velázquez, had
fallen into the hands of the wicked Giafar, who had once lost
a battle to him. To avenge himself Giafar had killed the seven
sons of Lara and had shown their heads to their father. After
being released from his prison, where he had met Zahira, Lara
had returned to Castile and had been thrown into jail as a
traitor by order of the Count of Castile, on the advice of Rui-
Velázquez.

Mudarra decides to avenge his father and his seven half-
brothers, and after writing a letter to Kerima, in which he
admits having killed Giafar, he leaves for Castile, accompanied
by Zaide. He reaches the castle of Lara and meets his old and
blind father who has been freed from jail after twenty years'
imprisonment following the death of the Count of Castile. Before the new Count of Castile, the great Fernán González,
Mudarra challenges Rui-Velázquez to single combat, but Rui-
Velázquez refuses to fight a bastard. Fernán González gives his
consent to the legitimization of the young man, and the duel
is fixed to take place in Burgos a month from the date.

We now learn something of the life of Rui-Velázquez. His
wife Doña Lambra had had an affair with a page and Rui-
Velázquez had killed the young man. He had imprisoned Doña
Lambra, but she had been able to escape to Galicia. Their young
son had burned to death in a fire in Rui-Velázquez' castle of
Barbadillo. The villain of the poem is afraid of the duel with
Mudarra and seeks the advice of a pious hermit. The latter

advises him to make reparation to those he had wronged, a suggestion which fills Rui-Velázquez with fury. He then goes to a wealthy abbot and is given assurance of victory after he decides to turn over his worldly possessions to the Abbey.

Finally the combat takes place, and Mudarra slays the wicked Rui-Velázquez. However, the victor receives a deep wound in his chest, and only thanks to the ministrations of Kerima, who had arrived from Cordova, does he recover. The two lovers are baptized and are about to be married when Kerima exclaims at the altar that she cannot marry her father's killer and that she will consecrate herself to God. The author then ends the poem by informing us that Mudarra married someone else and that the Manriques de Lara are his modern descendants.

IV *Influences and Sources*

Why did Saavedra choose to write such a long poem on the legend of the infantes of Lara? There were probably several factors behind his decision. Perhaps it was Saavedra's interest in medieval themes, an interest that had already shown itself in the composition of *El paso honroso* and *Florinda*, which prompted him to write on another medieval topic. Perhaps it was Saavedra's friend, John Hookham Frere, who had suggested, as Nicholson B. Adams indicates, that he write a poem in the general manner of Walter Scott's *The Lady of the Lake* or *Marmion*.[5] Doubtless the young poet's intensified interest in old Spanish ballads—there are many ballads on the subject of the seven *infantes* of Lara—, an interest spurred by Frere, had something to do with the composition of *The Foundling Moor*. Saavedra, who loved Cordova, may also have decided to write an epic poem contrasting his birthplace's erstwhile civilization with that of austere, tenth-century Castile. Another possibility is that Saavedra, who liked to write works which involved his own ancestors or those of friends, composed this poem in honor of his friend the Duke of Frías, a descendant of the Laras.

For a general influence on the composition of *El moro expósito* we should keep in mind Homer's epics and Virgil's *Aeneid*, with which Saavedra became acquainted in his years at the Seminario de Nobles, as well as the epic poems of Ariosto and

Tasso, although, as we shall see later, *El moro* moves away from the pattern of the traditional epic. More specifically, Saavedra may very well have read Juan de la Cueva's sixteenth-century play *Los siete infantes de Lara* and Lope de Vega's *El bastardo Mudarra y siete infantes de Lara*. As we have indicated above, he also read some of the old *romances*, or ballads, dealing with the legend. Furthermore, he knew Matos Fragoso's seventeenth-century play *Traidor contra su sangre y siete infantes de Lara* (*Traitor Against His Blood...*).[6] He certainly read José Antonio Conde's *Historia de la dominación de los árabes en España* (*History of the Domination of the Arabs in Spain*), which was published in three volumes in 1820–21 and enjoyed a considerable reputation in its day, although it has since been discredited. Finally, as Boussagol indicates, the influence of Madame Cottin's *Mathilde* may be behind the sentimentality which impregnates parts of the first five cantos.[7]

It would be tedious to discuss in detail the source of every single episode.[8] Let us mention the four principal sources the author himself mentions in his notes: Juan de Mariana's *Historia de España* (1601; Book VII, I, Chapter IX), Ambrosio de Morales' *Crónica general de España* (1574–86; Book XVII, Chapter XVI), Matos Fragoso's *Traidor contra su sangre y siete infantes de Lara*, and material given to him by his friend the Duke of Frías.

With respect to a few aspects, we shall only point to the idea that Mudarra is a foundling, which was probably suggested to Saavedra by Matos Fragoso;[9] to the moment when Kerima appears in the eleventh canto to help Mudarra, which was probably inspired by Saavedra's own *Florinda;* and to the final duel, for which the sources could have been Ginés Pérez de Hita's historical novel *Guerras civiles de Granada* (*Civil Wars of Granada;* 1595–1619), Nicolás Fernández de Moratín's eighteenth-century epic poem *Las naves de Cortés destruidas* (*The Destruction of the Ships of Cortés*),[10] Saavedra's own *Paso honroso*, and especially Walter Scott's *Ivanhoe*. Saavedra no doubt had read Walter Scott's immensely popular novel. Aside from the episode of the duel there are other similarities between the two works, such as *El moro*'s character of the worldly abbot, who resembles Scott's Prior of Jorvaulx.

Much of the traditional legend was modified by Saavedra when it suited his purpose. He built his poem around the figure of Mudarra, who thus becomes the central hero of the work at the expense of the *infantes* of Lara, whose fate is narrated by Zaide. Furthermore he refashioned the character of Mudarra, who in his sources is a "semi-barbaric, skull-splitting youth, all muscles and passion."[11] He also created a number of characters, including Giafar and Kerima. Although, as we have seen, there are many sources, these, to quote Nicholson B. Adams, "supplied Saavedra with only the bare bones of his poem, which he enriched with his own highly picturesque descriptions, which some find the most attractive feature of the composition."[12]

V   *The Problem of Genre*

Critics have had a good deal of difficulty in determining to what genre this work belongs. Saavedra himself adds after the title and subtitle the words "Leyenda en doce romances" ("Legend in Twelve Ballads"). The *leyenda*, a narrative in verse or prose relating a more or less fictional event or series of events, was developed as a genre in the nineteenth century,[13] and Saavedra was probably one of the first nineteenth-century Spanish authors to have used the term to label one of his poems. One might ask why Saavedra did not call this work a historical *romance* or ballad, since there may very well have been a historical basis to the story, and since he himself gave the title of *romances* to its twelve cantos. But, as Allison Peers rightly points out, *The Foundling Moor* has "little in common with the *romance*, which in general is more loosely built, carelessly told, and less purely literary in character."[14] We may add that the work is entirely too long to belong to the category of the ballad, a remark which also applies to the individual cantos, in spite of the title of *romance* which the author chose to give to each one of them. Could the poem have been inspired by the verse-narratives of Walter Scott? Peers thinks that this is "perhaps the nearest analogy that can be found to it."[15] Manuel Cañete, on the other hand, thought that it was unlike Scott's poetic novels such as *The Lady of the Lake* and that it would be more appropriate to call it a "leyenda épica," (an epic legend).[16] A nineteenth-century French critic, Charles de Mazade, wrote that *El moro* was at one and the same time a novel and a poem.[17] Menéndez Pidal declared that the work was "more a fictional legend than an epic poem,"[18] but Menéndez Pelayo, another famous Spanish scholar, expressed the opinion that it could be considered an epic poem.[19] Finally, Enrique Piñeyro, in his study of Spanish Romanticism, calls it a novel in verse.[20]

It seems to us that this unique work—which really has no precedent in Spanish literature and does not resemble anything written in Spain after it, in spite of its subtitle *leyenda*— partakes of both the epic and the novel. We agree with Peers that "the total effect produced by it is not epical" and that it does not have the over-all solemnity, simplicity, and grandeur of the true epic,[21] but it undeniably contains epic elements. At the same time there are aspects which are more characteristic of novelistic form. These two ingredients are ably combined and form a harmonious whole which leaves a pleasing effect on the reader in spite of the length of the work.

Among the epic ingredients let us first point to the presence of a hero who is dexterous, strong, courageous, and values his honor. After he is told of his origin he pursues unflinchingly one single goal, the avenging of his treacherously slain half-brothers. It would be an exaggeration to say, like the nineteenth-century novelist and critic Juan Valera, that Mudarra stands out among all the other characters like Achilles among the heroes of Homer,[22] especially since, as we shall see later, there are definite Romantic qualities about him which modify the traditional epic image. But Mudarra is sufficiently pure in heart and sufficiently valiant to be classified an epic hero, even if he is somewhat removed from the heroes of Homer.[23] Underlining his epic aspect the author speaks thus of Mudarra after his victory:

El vencedor gallardo, el hijo suyo,	The brave victor, his son,
a quien después de Dios lo debe todo;	To whom, after God, he owes everything;
el héroe triunfador, cuyo denuedo	The triumphant hero, whose courage
derribar pudo al bárbaro coloso	Was able to demolish the barbarous colossus,

de calumnia y traición que le oprimía,	Filled with calumny and treason, who persecuted him,
y deshacerlo en ignominia y polvo,	And reduce him to ignominy and dust,
y a Castilla, y a España, y a la tierra	And free Castile and Spain and the earth
libres dejar de tan horrendo monstruo. . . .	From such a horrendous monster.[24]

The remaining "good" characters are, like Mudarra, very good. On the other hand we have some grandiose villains. Giafar, the father of Kerima, and especially Rui-Velázquez, who finally succumbs in an epic clash of arms, have no redeeming features. Even the villainy of Doña Lambra, the wife of Rui-Velázquez, has an epic quality.[25] This is the way Saavedra describes her:

> She was a sepulcher of shining marble,
> A prison of corruption and of worms;
> She was a beautiful palace, where shone
> The burnished bronze and the chiseled jasper,
>
> Of sublime proportion, enriched
> With columns, reliefs and foliages;
> Inhabited by furious hyenas,
> Hungry wolves and enraged dogs. (p. 217)

Epic scenes abound. Let us mention for instance the episode in the third *romance*, related to Mudarra by Zaide, of the bad omens in the castle of Lara, with their tragic implications, when Lara's escutcheon crashes to the ground and when the youngest son of Lara, Gonzalo, knocks over a saltshaker to the consternation of all those present. In the course of the festivities attendant upon the marriage of Rui-Velázquez and Doña Lambra the same Gonzalo vanquishes Doña Lambra's cousin, the gigantic Alvaro Sánchez, in single combat. The clash between the seemingly invincible giant and his valiant opponent, with the accompanying suspense and the uncommon skill and courage which is ascribed to the smaller man, has a decidedly epic quality about it. Epic, too, in all its horror is the scene, derived from

the original legend, in which Gonzalo Gustios is presented with
the heads of his murdered sons and in which he addresses each
of the heads by name. The prophecy by which Rui-Velázquez
is told in the ninth canto to beware of the scimitar of Almanzor,
is a frequent device of the epic. So is the figure of the saintly
hermit who advises Rui-Velázquez to beg his enemies for forgiveness. And epic of course is the momentous clash between
Mudarra and Rui-Velázquez, in which the latter loses his life.

Next to these epic moments there are many others that could
be characterized as novelistic. Such is the whole episode of
the sixth canto which speaks of the feast which was prepared
in the home of the archpriest. The author describes painstak-
ingly the various activities supervised by the housekeeper, including the killing and plucking of the chickens, the seasoning of a
stew, and the opening of the wine cellar. Even some light
mischief claims the attention of the poet: An old woman,
circumventing the vigilance of the housekeeper's niece, succeeds
in slipping a sausage into her apron; another grabs a sirloin,
and a boy dips his finger into the honey, while his friend drinks
brandy from a jug (p. 172).

The realism of the whole scene reminds us of the novels of
Walter Scott. The same can be said of the comic scene in the
seventh canto, in which the drunken ex-houndkeeper of the
house of Lara, Vasco Pérez, mistakes Mudarra for one of the
seven dead sons of Gonzalo Gustios and, as the author delicately
puts it, "fell to the ground, / And watered it with wine which /
he had drunk the previous night" (p. 189).[26] Vasco Pérez'
character is further developed in the eighth canto, where we
learn that he possesses many skills, including that of singing,
and where he serves as a guide to Mudarra. A good example of
how the epic and a realism more characteristic of the novel are
combined in this work is the previously mentioned episode of the
seven severed heads. After addressing each of the heads, Gonzalo Gustios kisses the cheek of the youngest son and, overcome
by the cold of the flesh and by the revolting odor, faints. The
head then falls on his chest and from there rolls on the carpet,
"leaving a dirty track / Of congealed blood, putrid and black"
(p. 148).

Finally, among the non-epic, novelistic passages, worthy of

note is the visit in the tenth canto of Rui-Velázquez to the accommodating abbot. The latter is described in great detail:

> In his sixties, but robust;
> Of medium size, of pronounced obesity,
> Of affected gravity, of slow gait,
> Of strong but laborious breathing.
>
> His eyes are gay and vivacious;
> His fresh and round face exudes health,
> And his wide, ruddy cheeks
> And his nose, red at the tip,
>
> Indicate that savory, succulent
> And abundant dishes are his fare,
> And that his digestion is always helped
> By wines of old vintage and great potency and aroma. (p. 243)

The cautious and worldly abbot, who agrees to have prayers said in return for the gifts Rui-Velázquez will make to the Abbey, is a finely chiseled character; he is accompanied by three equally worldly monks who are described with the same irony. This irony, as well as some other instances of slight anti-clerical barbs in *El moro expósito*,[27] caused raised eyebrows among some Spanish critics, and some charges of anticlericalism were made against the poet. Anticipating these accusations, Saavedra appended a long footnote to this passage, insisting that it was not his intention to satirize the monastic state, "but to paint the customs of the tenth century" and to present the monkish gluttony and moral laxity which were known to have been widespread in the Middle Ages (p. 246, n.). Be that as it may, it is entirely possible that the whole episode, together with other jabs at churchmen found in the poem, reflects to some extent a slight anticlericalism which could very well have been part of Saavedra's *Weltanschauung* at the time he wrote *El moro expósito*. Saavedra was still a liberal, and anticlericalism usually went hand in hand with liberalism. Moreover, since the description of the abbot and his companions occurs in the tenth canto, which was completed in Paris in 1832, we may surmise that it reflects perhaps the additional ideological influence of the poet's friend, the liberal Alcalá Galiano, who in those days was a constant companion of the future Duke.

VI Romantic Traits

In an unsigned review of *El moro expósito* which appeared in the *Revista Española* in May, 1834, the anonymous author[28] asserted that the work was not "an essentially Romantic composition," for it lacked certain specifically Romantic elements such as the "metaphysical slant, the nebulous concepts and the fantastic pictures of those who walk the path of exclusive Romanticism." On the other hand the poem could not be termed Neoclassical, for the "rigid supporters of Horace and Boileau will reject it almost in its entirety, terming it spurious and monstrous." For the author the work presents a new and essentially Spanish type of Romanticism: "We believe that [Saavedra] is not an exact reflection of the English, German, or French Romantics; but we do think that he naturalizes the genre . . . , giving it a Spanish appearance."[29]

Indeed the poet, as he had done in the earlier *Paso honroso* and *Florinda*, has chosen in *El moro expósito* a subject matter taken from the Spanish national tradition and based to a considerable extent on Spanish popular and literary sources; he has presented a very Spanish story. In the words of the anonymous critic of the *Revista Española* there are to be found in this work "a good imprint of our best poets, reminiscences of their turns of phrases, of their images, their elegance. . . ."[30] He has eschewed some of the more extreme traits of European Romanticism. The hero is not a rebel against God and society. He is not an idealist who fights desperately against a prosaic reality only to find disillusion. His love is powerful, but it is not a passion that leads to suicide. In this connection it is interesting to recall that at the end Kerima does not marry Mudarra, and neither Kerima nor Mudarra die of grief or commit suicide.[31] Mudarra recovers after the blow and eventually marries someone else. The end is perhaps tragic, but it is not Romantic.

While avoiding some Romantic exaggerations found in European literature, Saavedra has used a number of Romantic ingredients such as the horrible, as we have seen for instance in the episode of the head of the youngest Lara, and the grotesque, as for instance in the episode of the drunk Vasco Pérez.[32] He has also employed the device of antithesis, as we shall see shortly.

Mudarra himself has some characteristics normally associated with Romantic heroes. At the beginning, a mystery hangs like a veil over his origin, and this mystery, coupled with the death of his protectress (actually his mother) Zahira, makes him brood and walk about alone among the crowds during the festivities in Cordova. In the following lines the poet also mentions a terrible destiny which weighs on him, another element which often accompanies the Romantic hero: "He thinks about his humiliating, obscure origin; / He thinks of Zahira, and he thinks that he is called / By a terrible destiny, more terrible / Because of the mystery which shrouds and protects it" (p. 105). But there is more than destiny involved. If we read the poem carefully we realize that Saavedra is telling us that Mudarra's destiny is only an aspect of Divine Providence which determines throughout the poem the events taking place in Cordova and Burgos and especially the actions of Mudarra.[33] Let us but think of the failure of the attempt on Mudarra's life early in the poem, of the domestic unhappiness of Rui-Velázquez, of the loss of his son, of Mudarra's victory over his enemy, and of the refusal of Kerima, remembering the death of her father at the hands of her lover, to marry the hero.[34] In the seventh *romance*, when old Gustios de Lara recognizes in the Moorish warrior his only remaining son, he indicates clearly the role which Mudarra is to play: "Are you, oh young man!, / The executor of God's ire?" (p. 192). And Zaide then tells Gustios:

> "Recognize
> Oh great Lara!, the one in your arms
> As the messenger from the Author of the world.
>
> He sends him to you to demonstrate to the world
> That He never leaves unpunished
> Atrocious crimes, and that his eternal justice
> Always provides innocence with avengers. (p. 192)

Ángel Crespo has shown convincingly the importance of Providence in the structure of the poem and has pointed out that Mudarra is a new phenomenon in Spanish literature: according to the Spanish critic he is the "hero of Providence."[35]

Like many Romantic heroes Mudarra is quite emotional. In the first *romance* he is upset at having forgotten temporarily about his origin and about Zahira: "He thinks, oh unfortunate one!, that the shadow / Of Zahira follows him and threatens him, / And that he is harassed and surrounded / By specters and ghosts." Whereupon he strikes quite a Romantic pose: "He leans his back against a solitary trunk; / Bereft of his strength in such a great storm; / Fighting for breath, he crosses his arms on his chest, / He lowers his head and, grieving, remains speechless" (p. 106). After he kills Giafar in self-defense he runs to Zaide: "He raises his head, emits a moan, and says: / 'I have killed the father of Kerima.' / And with renewed terror he tries to hide / In the friendly arms of the tender Zaide" (p. 126).

The melancholy and the emotionalism displayed by Mudarra are particularly marked in the first four cantos, before the departure of the young foundling and Zaide. But they do not disappear in the cantos which see Mudarra in Castile. In the seventh *romance*, for instance, Mudarra, seeing his father overcome with joy at meeting him, to the point of actually fainting, hides in the arms of Zaide, "full of terror" (p. 191). And in the last *romance*, when seeing off Zaide, who is returning to Cordova, the young man is bathed in tears (p. 265).

Episodes that must be termed Romantic abound in the work. In the second *romance*, for instance, Mudarra visits the grave of Zahira and at one point imagines that he is surrounded by grim ghosts. He flees from that spot and the author, apostrophizing Mudarra and Kerima, somberly tells them that immense obstacles await them: "It seems that the voice of the other world / Is repeating to you inexorably: / That a sea of blood is roaring between you two, / That there is a wall of unburied bones" (p. 119). Shortly the two lovers meet at the tomb and solemnly declare their love for each other:

> Their simple souls declared
> The mutual flame in which they burned;

And with gentle tears they swore
Eternal love in spite of Fate;
And the tomb was the altar of their love. . . . (p. 120)

This whole episode is, as Gabriel Boussagol points out, one of those manifestations of the poetry of night and tombs which was dear to eighteenth-century pre-Romantics.[36] We might add that the seting was also a favorite with the Romantics.

In the fifth canto, Kerima, filled with grief after discovering that Mudarra had killed her father, wanders about in the mountains in the midst of a terrible storm, which forms a perfect backdrop to her desperation, a typically Romantic feature. In the eighth canto Vasco Pérez, the houndkeeper, is attacked by two assassins, armed with daggers, who mistake him for Mudarra. After this attempt at assassination fails, poison is tried, but again the plot ends in failure and, instead of Mudarra, it is a dog that dies. These two motifs of the dagger and the poison "seem to have passed from the French Romantic drama—which the author sees performed in Paris—to the modern Spanish epic."[37] Finally, let us point to the scene in the eleventh canto, when the old hag Elvida calls out to Rui-Velázquez, who has just knocked Mudarra from his horse, asking him whether he does not see the seven ghosts of the infantes of Lara who are helping Mudarra in his life-and-death struggle; she screeches out the following song:

The traitor, the murderer
Is surrounded by a sea of blood.
His unburied victims
Drown him in the waves.

Hell opens its mouth
To swallow him. . . . Do they not hear
The cries of the demons
With which they greet such a guest? (p. 256)

This unexpected intervention of the half-crazed old woman, the reference to the ghosts of the infantes, and the sinister song create a grotesque and at the same time chilling effect which must have pleased the most ardent Romantics of Saavedra's times.

In the preface to *El moro expósito*, Alcalá Galiano mentions that Saavedra has broken certain rules. These are of course the rules of Neoclassic art. For one thing, Saavedra does not observe in his long poem the rule of not mixing the sublime and the humble, as recommended by the eighteenth-century Spanish Neoclassic theoretician Ignacio de Luzán. Luzán recommends that if the poet describes a magnificent palace he should not enter at the same time chophouses or stables. Saavedra does precisely something similar to this when he speaks of the preparations for the feast in the kitchen of the archpriest's house after having recounted the triumphant return of the old and blind Gustios de Lara to his castle. Saavedra also goes against the Neoclassic injunction not to mingle the comic and the tragic. In presenting both tragic and comic as well as grotesque episodes in this poem, he follows the example set by European, especially French, Romanticism, but also by Shakespeare and above all by the Spanish playwrights of the seventeenth century.

The sublime and the humble, the tragic and the comic are some of the pillars of the device of contrast which is dear to the Romantic poet and of which Saavedra makes use in this work. We have the contrast between the "good" and the "bad" characters. In the case of one "bad" character we have the contrast between moral and physical characteristics: While an evil woman, Doña Lambra is also a beautiful one: "Beautiful, although the fresh luster / Of first youth had passed.... / But the heart of Doña Lambra was composed of infernal poisons..." (pp. 216–17). There is also the contrast between the saintly hermit and the worldly abbot. But where Saavedra takes full advantage of the Romantic device of antithesis is in the descriptions of Cordova and Burgos. We must keep in mind that the subtitle of this work is *Cordova and Burgos in the Tenth Century*. The contrast between these two cities, symbolizing the contrast between Moorish and Christian civilizations, plays an important role in the poem. Cordova, Saavedra's birthplace, is presented as a majestic town, a center of wealth and culture, watered by a magnificent river, the Guadalquivir, and set in a smiling countryside:

Era en aquella edad Córdoba insigne	In those days Cordova was a famous
de los placeres y riquezas centro,	Center of pleasure and wealth,
y en la alta cumbre, de esplendor y gloria,	And on the high summit of splendor and glory
resplandecía el musulmán imperio.	Shone the Moslem empire.
Las artes, el saber y la opulencia,	The arts, knowledge, and opulence
de la hermosa ciudad su trono hicieron,	Made their throne in the beautiful city,
a la par que el valor y la fortuna	While valor and fortune
la adornaban de triunfos y trofeos.	Adorned it with triumphs and trophies. (p. 120)

Cordova, i.e., Moslem Spain, is splendid and powerful. Yet Saavedra notes that it is about to begin its decline. On the other hand Burgos, i.e., Christian Spain, is poor and ignorant; but it has an inner strength which will soon mean a decisive advantage over the Moslem rival. To Saavedra, the son of the south, Burgos and Castile form a harsh contrast with his beloved Cordova. Castile has a "horizon of horrid mountains" and a barren soil where only black-green pines flourish. The waters of the Arlanza, river of Burgos, run muddy and sluggish; and the heavens, dark with stubborn clouds, are contrasted with the "sapphire sky" of Cordova. Burgos shows "thick walls and towers / Of rough stone, where the sun does not shine" (p. 166), and the sounds which one hears there are mostly those of church bells, of hammers striking anvils, and of choirs singing monotonously in monasteries, convents, and churches (p. 167).

It has been said that Saavedra did not depict Cordova and Burgos and their customs with historical accuracy and that he committed a number of anachronisms. This criticism is justified; but Saavedra, in spite of the use which he made of various sources—among these, Conde's book on the Arab domination in Spain was not very accurate—was not particularly interested in an archaeological reconstruction of Spain in the tenth century. Besides, it did not matter to nineteenth-century readers that the color lavished on Cordova and Burgos was not historically accurate. The poet used his imagination and used it well and convincingly. No matter how little the author of *El moro* knew about the actual history and the manners and customs of all parts of Spain at that epoch, his picture is artistically valid. Ten centuries after that time the modern tourist is quite likely to agree with Saavedra. Andalusia in general and Cordova in particular possess a charm through natural surroundings and tradition that is very different from the stern though admirable qualities of the northern province.

The picturesqueness and the local color dear to Romanticism which Saavedra achieves in this poem are due to a certain extent to his use of light and color. Saavedra the painter had been drawn from his earliest days to these two qualities, but in *El moro expósito* he uses them more than in previous works. While Saavedra uses primary colors—red, green, a bit of yellow (including gold) and a suggestion of violet—we should mention especially the constant use of white and the effects of light and shade.

The references to light and whiteness are very numerous: Zahira is beautiful as the "gleaming day star" (p. 98), despite her melancholy. The dream of Lara in his jail is filled with the impression of light, and when, in the company of his old friend and retainer Nuño, he settles again in his palace near Burgos, he rejoices in the warmth of the sunlight which he can no longer see. In the final episode, floods of light bathe Burgos: "Spreading its resplendent torrent, / The immense sun, generator of gold, / Moved through empty space / To occupy the high throne of the zenith" (p. 268).

The images involving whiteness begin in the third quatrain of Canto I: "The moon, of gleaming mother-of-pearl / Shines on the sea amid light clouds" (p. 97). White predominates in the description of the wedding of Almanzor's son Abdimelik to Habiba. The hundred horsemen who are relatives of the groom wear scarlet, tight-fitting garments, but white turbans, and ride horses "white as foam" (p. 101). Saavedra usually gives the color of horses, and he does so throughout *El moro expósito*. We are not surprised that Kerima and the nineteen virgins with her should be dressed in white linen robes which reach to their feet. In the last canto, in the scene marking the reception into the Christian faith of Kerima and Mudarra, the principals are dressed in white. The youths in the procession have white banners and red plumes, and the knights and nobles white ribbons hanging from their shoulders.

In Castile, snow covers the mountains. White mists may cover the woods. It is not remarkable that the hair and beards of Gonzalo Gustios and other old men should be white. We might expect Kerima's skin to be at least slightly swarthy, but no, her face and neck are entirely white, and her countenance seems to be of jasmine and of roses, contrasting with her black eyelashes and hair. The description of Rui-Velázquez' wife is remarkably similar: "Her mouth was pearls and corals, / Her eyes two gleaming stars, / Her face snow and roses, / Her long tresses . . . of jet . . . / Her throat and breasts / Seemed burnished alabaster . . . / Her delicate hands, of jasmine . . ." (p. 217). Those are only a few of the references to whiteness scattered throughout the long poem.

Not everything is Romantic in *El moro expósito.* Alcalá Galiano is generally right when he states that Saavedra has not used Classical and mythological allusions in this poem.[38] Nonetheless, a few Classical procedures can be found in *El moro.* "Some whole lines have a sonorous classic ring, as have various expressions and single words. We observe periphrases for expressions of time according to the sun or the moon, twenty springs or twenty winters for twenty years, according to the models which the poet had previously followed."[39] Saavedra's description of spring in Castile, for instance, toward the end of the poem, is quite Neoclassic. He uses conventional terms in speaking of the "invierno aterido" (numb winter), "apacible primavera" (peaceful spring), "dulces tomillos" (sweet thyme), "plácidos arroyos" (placid streams), and Favonio or zephyr—in other words, expressions we would expect in such eighteenth-century poets as Meléndez Valdés.

The meter employed throughout is the eleven-syllable, assonant *romance heroico*,[40] and we do not have the metrical variety that is so often found in Romantic poems. Alcalá Galiano states in the prologue that this verse form had rarely or never been used in long works. That it had never been used in long works is true, but it had been employed by the eighteenth-century Neoclassic playwright García de la Huerta in his tragedy *Raquel* (1778), by the Neoclassic poet Quintana in his tragedy *Pelayo*

64   THE DUKE OF RIVAS

(1805), and by the Neoclassic *par excellence*, Leandro Fernández de Moratín in his poem *La toma de Granada* (*The Capture
of Granada*).[41] This meter strikes the ear as somewhat monoto-
nous, and at times the poem reads practically like prose. Some
of the blame for this must be placed on the many overlaps we
find in the verses. However, we should also note that this last
feature could be termed Romantic, since it indicates a departure
from Neoclassic theory, which among so many other things
forbade overlaps in poetry.[42]

VII *Conclusion*

This then is the work which thanks to some of the characteristics of the hero, to the uses of contrast, to its picturesqueness,
etc., permitted Spanish Romanticism to come into its own. No
matter how many sources Saavedra may have utilized, and
granted that the basis for the plot was the age-old legend of
the infantes of Lara, the end product—and let us keep in mind
that this is a poem of more than 14,000 lines—is still a highly
original work, written with zest and vigor, and relating a tragic
story of great sweep and color. Cordova and Burgos are brilliantly contrasted, and in the hero Mudarra the author effectively
blends the qualities that he may very well have thought
characteristic of both Andalusia and Castile—valor, skill in the
handling of arms, a capacity for great passion, and above all,
determination.

As in all literary works, there are flaws. The character of
Mudarra, in spite of all his qualities, could have been given
sharper contours. At times he seems to be a less vivid personage
than Rui-Velázquez or even Giafar and Gustios de Lara. In
addition, Kerima's personality arouses no particular interest in
the reader. She disappears from sight at the end of the fifth canto
and is not seen again until the eleventh canto, thus creating a
sentimental gap in the poem. There are digressions that are too
long, and there are signs indicating that the end was perhaps
written somewhat carelessly and in a hurry. But the over-all
impression is nevertheless that of a masterpiece which fully
deserved the favorable reception it was accorded on publication
and which deserves to be read much more often and much more
widely than is the case today.

CHAPTER 4

Rivas' Excursion into Super-Romanticism: Don Alvaro o la fuerza del sino

I *The Plot*

R IVAS' most important play, his one excursion into what
we might call super-Romanticism, was performed in Madrid
on March 22, 1835, opening the way for the brief blossoming
of French style Romantic drama in Spain; it consists of five
jornadas or acts, written in verse and prose. At the beginning
of the play the action is situated in and near Seville in the
1740's. Don Alvaro, the son of a Spanish viceroy and an Inca
princess, has gone to Spain to obtain a royal pardon for his
parents, who have been imprisoned in Peru for having plotted
to set up an independent monarchy. In Seville he has fallen
in love with Doña Leonor, the daughter of the Marquis of
Calatrava. The latter has refused him the girl's hand and has
taken her to a country house near Seville. Don Alvaro then
tries to elope with her. As he is about to carry out his plan,
the hero is surprised by the Marquis, who has been warned
that the young man might make such a rash move. Don Alvaro
kneels before Calatrava and declares his readiness to die at
his hands. As he throws down his pistol, it fires and mortally
wounds the Marquis, who before dying curses his daughter.
Don Alvaro, wounded in the ensuing struggle between his
servants and those of Calatrava, is separated from Doña Leonor,
whom he subsequently believes to be dead. He later joins the
Spanish army in Italy, hoping to die in battle. Doña Leonor,
after spending a year with her aunt in Cordova, begins the
life of a hermit near a monastery in the mountains above
Hornachuelos, not far from Cordova.

65

In Italy Don Carlos, the older son of the Marquis, looking
for the man who has been the cause of his father's death and
his sister's "dishonor," becomes the friend of an incognito Don
Alvaro. But while Don Alvaro recovers from wounds received
in a battle against the Austrians, Don Carlos finds the portrait
of his sister among his friend's belongings and realizes that he
has found the man for whom he is looking. After he has re-
covered, Don Alvaro is challenged to a duel by Don Carlos,
and although he tries to avoid this confrontation, the other's
intransigence leaves him no choice. Don Alvaro kills Don Carlos
and is about to be condemned to death by virtue of a law
recently promulgated by King Charles of Naples,[1] which orders
the death penalty for dueling. But he is saved by an Austrian
attack which catches the Spanish forces by surprise in the
town where he is jailed.

Don Alvaro then returns to Spain and becomes a monk in
the monastery near which Leonor lives as a hermit; he is of
course unaware that he is now so close to his beloved. Four
years later, Don Alfonso, Don Carlos' younger brother, finds
him there and challenges him to a duel. Don Alvaro again tries
to appease his enemy, but upon being struck in the face and
insulted by the latter, he inflicts a mortal wound on his tor-
mentor. Don Alfonso asks for confession and Don Alvaro,
considering himself unworthy of administering confession to
the dying man, knocks on the door of the hermitage, which
happens to be near the place where they have fought. Doña
Leonor appears at the door and as she falls into the arms of
her brother, the latter, thinking that she had been all the time
together with Don Alvaro, kills her with his dagger. The desperate Don Alvaro climbs atop a crag and before the horrified
eyes of the monks who have come to the spot where the killings
have taken place, invites hell to receive him and plunges over
a precipice.

II *Influences and Sources*

In general terms, the Romantic plays Rivas saw in Paris must
have made a strong impression on him and probably induced
him to write a play which might create as much of a stir on

the French stage as Hugo's *Hernani* or Dumas' *Antony*. In this connection let us recall that Alcalá Galiano translated the first version into French for performance in a Paris theater.

For the basic plot Rivas very possibly made use of some stories, traditions, or legends of his native Cordova which he had heard as a child. There may very well have been a story about a mestizo or a mulatto who had fallen in love with a Spanish girl from an aristocratic family and had come to a tragic end.[2] Perhaps, too, a model for Don Alvaro may be found in the famous writer Garcilaso de la Vega, surnamed El Inca (1539–1616), illegitimate son of a Spanish soldier and an Inca princess, who had been a soldier and later a priest and who was buried in the Cathedral of Cordova.[3] Moreover, Rivas obviously knew the story of the *mujer penitente* (the penitent woman) who was supposed to have spent ten years in a grotto or cave near the monastery of Los Angeles above Hornachuelos in the last years of the fifteenth century.[4]

Some critics have pointed to the influence of Byron. There is some resemblance between Byron's Lara and Don Alvaro, and the latter's search for death also recalls Byron's Manfred, who, like Don Alvaro, has vainly courted death: "I have affronted death—but in the war / Of elements the waters shrunk from me, / And fatal things pass'd harmless."[5]

Boussagol points to Tirso de Molina's *El burlador de Sevilla* (*The Trickster of Seville*), to Guillén de Castro's *Las mocedades del Cid* (*The Feats of the Young Cid*), and the author's own *El moro expósito*, in all of which the father of a beloved young woman is killed, as possibly inspiring the scene of the death of Doña Leonor's father.[6] It is also possible that the eighteenth-century play *El delincuente honrado* (*The Honorable Culprit*) by Gaspar Melchor de Jovellanos, in which the hero is condemned to death for having killed a man in an illegal duel, inspired *Don Alvaro*'s fourth act, when the hero is arrested for the death by dueling of Don Carlos.[7] Furthermore, there are some slight similarities with Alexandre Dumas' *Antony* and *Don Juan de Marana*.[8]

The greatest problem in connection with the question of sources arises because of the similarities between *Don Alvaro* and *Les âmes du Purgatoire* (*The Souls of Purgatory*) by the

French writer Prosper Mérimée. In Mérimée's novel a young man, Don Juan, is surprised one night in the room of a girl, Doña Fausta, by her father Don Alfonso de Ojeda. Don Juan kills him, joins the army, goes to Flanders, returns to Spain, and enters a monastery. The brother of Doña Fausta, Don Pedro, finds him there and strikes his face to force him to fight. Don Juan kills Don Pedro.

Leopoldo Augusto de Cueto, Rivas' brother-in-law, declares in his *Discurso necrológico* that Rivas almost certainly received from the French novel the "embryo" of his dramatic work.[9] Other critics dispute this. They emphasize the fact that *Les âmes du Purgatoire* began to appear in the *Revue des Deux Mondes* on August 15, 1834, while *Don Alvaro* was finished at Tours, France in 1832 or 1833. True, this was the first version, in prose, of the Spanish play, which was later transformed to a large extent into verse by Rivas upon his return to Spain.[10] But the writer Ramón de Mesonero Romanos, to whom Rivas read several scenes in Paris in 1833, mentions no difference between the play performed in 1835 and the earlier manuscript.[11] Moreover, it appears that Mérimée saw the first version after it had been translated into French by Alcalá Galiano and was thus able, if he chose to do so, to draw on it for inspiration for his own novel.[12]

There is also some internal evidence that Mérimée may well have been the one to do the borrowing rather than Rivas. The most striking similarity lies in the provocation scenes. As Boussagol notes, if we accept the idea that Rivas borrowed the provocation in the fifth act from Mérimée, then we also have to accept the idea that he altered his first manuscript in order to make all of Don Alvaro's reactions to Leonor's relatives similar. For Don Alvaro has the same attitude and the same feelings upon each meeting with a male member of the Calatrava family (for instance, he goes down on his knees both in the first and fifth acts), attitude and feelings which are the mark of his character. But it is difficult to imagine that this total conception could derive from the dénouement in Mérimée, which is only an episode, not an essential part of his plot.[13] Mérimée's work could easily have had another ending, while *Don Alvaro* has to end the way it does. It seems more than possible, then, that Mérimée derived some of his material from Rivas.[14]

It has finally been suggested that the Romantic drama *Elena* by the playwright Bretón de los Herreros might have served as an inspiration for *Don Alvaro.*[15] *Elena*, which was performed on October 23, 1834, is melodramatic enough, but we fail to see in this story of a couple separated until their final reunion by the machinations of the heroine's uncle, who is in love with her, any meaningful similarity with *Don Alvaro*. True, destiny is mentioned a number of times; the lovers seem pursued by a hostile fate; Elena seeks refuge in the countryside; and the fourth act takes place in a craggy landscape. But the plot and the motivations of the characters of *Don Alvaro* make this a play vastly different from *Elena*.

III   Don Alvaro, *the Super-Romantic Drama*

With *Don Alvaro* Rivas introduced to the Spanish stage a play that in its boldness of conception and execution went far beyond the steps taken by Martínez de la Rosa and Larra in their *La conjuración de Venecia* and *Macías* respectively. Here was a play that could compare its revolt against Neoclassic precepts with that of Victor Hugo's *Hernani* and *Lucrèce Borgia* (1833) as well as with that of Dumas' *Antony*. *Don Alvaro* has all the trappings of what we could call a super-Romantic play. First, we have the basic theme, the triumph of fate over love, which is also found in other full-blown Romantic dramas like *Hernani*. As Donald Shaw notes, it is "the basic theme of all the major Spanish Romantic dramas."[16] Next, there is a hero who brings to mind the great heroes of Byron or Hugo, a Lara or a Manfred, an Hernani or a Ruy Blas. From the very beginning, through the conversation of a number of persons gathered in Seville at a stall for serving water, we are given to understand that he is handsome, rich, and generous, that he excels at bull-fighting, and that he is a fine swordsman. Later his prowess with the sword is shown through his two victories over the brothers Calatrava, one of whom, we are told in Act I, scene 2, is an extremely dangerous duelist. Don Alvaro's prowess in battle, though caused essentially by his desire to find death on the battlefield, becomes legendary and he is known in the Spanish army in Italy as "la prez de España" (the glory of Spain).

There is an aura of pessimism about him, caused of course by the unfortunate circumstances that surround him and have surrounded him since his birth. This pessimism, this melancholy, this Romantic *mal du siècle*, which we find in other Romantic heroes, is indicated to us by the author when he describes Don Alvaro, entering in Act I, scene 3, as "looking with dignity and melancholy toward all sides."[17] His deep pessimism is especially manifest in Act III, scene 3, when he complains about the injustice of fate and his inability to find death.

The Romantic hero is capable of great passion. Don Alvaro is passionately in love with Doña Leonor who fully returns his love. He is highly emotional, capable of moving in an instant from one emotional extreme to the other. When in Act I, scene 7, Doña Leonor tells him they should leave the elopement for the next day, he gives vent to his despair:

Me sacarán difunto	I shall be carried out dead
de aquí cuando inmortal salir creía.	From here when I thought I would leave immortal.
Hechicera engañosa,	Deceitful sorceress,
¿la perspectiva hermosa	Do you thus undo
que falaz me ofreciste así deshaces?	The beautiful future Which you treacherously offered me?
¡Pérfida! ¿Te complaces	Perfidious one! Do you take pleasure
en levantarme al trono del Eterno	In raising me up to the throne of God
para después hundirme en el infierno?	In order later to hurl me down into hell? (p. 312)

Allison Peers claims that in the last scene of the first act, Rivas ruins the impression his hero has made so far by having Don Alvaro behave in a decidedly non-heroic way in kneeling before the Marquis of Calatrava and offering him his life.[18] But is this really a flaw? Would Don Alvaro have produced a more heroic impression if he had killed the Marquis or one or more of the latter's servants? It seems to us, on the contrary, that this is logical behavior for a man whose nobility of character has been emphasized up to now.

A further Romantic element in the personality of the hero is the veil of mystery which hangs over him from the beginning of the play. We are given to understand in the first act that Indian blood flows in his veins, and we are given more details of his background in Don Alvaro's soliloquy of Act III, scene 3. But it is not until the very end that we are told by Don Alfonso the full story of Don Alvaro's family. Thus the mystery is kept alive until the very last moment.[19]

By virtue of his Indian blood Don Alvaro is a mestizo. Thus we have in this play an exotic ingredient sure to appeal to European Romanticism. Moreover this racial factor plays a certain role in the action. We would not go as far as Walter T. Pattison, who suggests that Don Alvaro suffers from a complex, an inability to face the fact of his mixed blood, which actually prevents him from seeking the freedom of his parents, and that "his unwillingness to tell his secret [his mixed blood] is the key to his psychology, his fate, and the structure of the play."[20] We doubt that Rivas would wish to give his hero such a complex character, judging from the totality of his work, which does not reveal a strong interest in exploring the inner recesses of the mind.[21] Moreover, in the words of Richard Cardwell, "this type of Freudian analysis not only overlooks the fact that Rivas chose to subtitle the play *la fuerza del sino*, it also underrates Rivas' intention to demonstrate that some force, which he chose to call *sino*, can be seen at work exerting its power over the hero Don Alvaro."[22] We feel that Don Alvaro's explanation that he had not revealed his background upon arriving in Spain because his name had a criminal taint (Act III, sc. 3) is sufficient to explain his silence on this point without bringing in his mixed blood. As for his failure to work for the liberation of his parents, we must keep in mind that the death of the Marquis and the loss of Doña Leonor had such an impact on him that he could think of nothing but seeking death in battle. Again, after Carlos' death and his escape from jail he was in no condition psychologically to work for his parents' release and was fit only to retire from the world.

On the other hand, that Don Alvaro has a certain sensitivity to his racial background cannot be denied. It is a fact that when confronted with this problem he is capable of reacting violently. These reactions, together with his pride in his royal Inca ancestry, clearly underline the exotic side of his personality.[23] In the last act Brother Melitón relates to the prior of the monastery that when he told Padre Rafael—that is, Don Alvaro—that he looked like a mulatto, the latter made a fist and raised it, without striking him, however. On another occasion, when Melitón suggested jokingly to Padre Rafael that he looked like a wild Indian, the Padre bellowed at him. When Don Alfonso asks Don Alvaro maliciously whether his family escutcheon is not tainted by any mixed, impure blood, Don Alvaro, beside himself with rage, explodes: "You lie, you lie, you scoundrel! / Give me the sword, my fury / Will tear out your tongue, / Which insults my pure lineage" (p. 359). Finally, Don Alvaro kills Don Alfonso when the latter calls him a "mestizo, a fruit of treason" (p. 362).

When Melitón speaks of Don Alvaro to the Prior he not only mentions his "Indian" and "mulatto" aspect but also a behavior which strikes him as demonic (p. 354). We are given to understand on several occasions that there is something diabolical about Don Alvaro. In Act I, scene 4, one character of the group around the water stall says that he saw Don Alvaro pass by him "like a soul taken away by demons" (p. 306). In the last act we have the above-mentioned remark of Melitón and the statement of Don Alfonso to Melitón identifying Don Alvaro as "the one from hell" (p. 355); Don Alvaro's answer to Melitón's question as to where he is going with Don Alfonso: "I am going to hell" (p. 359); Melitón's remark as he sees Don Alvaro and Don Alfonso hurry through the mountains: "They are devils, that is clear" (p. 360), and finally Don Alvaro's words before he jumps over the precipice: "I am an envoy from hell, I am the exterminating demon" (p. 363).[24] Rivas partook of the Romantic tendency to attribute demonic qualities to literary or historical figures. Certain Satanic aspects are often found in Romantic villains and even heroes. In the words of Van Tieghem, "the Cursed one symbolizes various anxieties, various Romantic protests, or simply incarnates Evil or Misfortune."[25] Among the many examples we might cite the protagonist of the

Spanish poet José de Espronceda's *El estudiante de Salamanca*
(*The Student of Salamanca*), a Don Juan figure, who is called
a "grandiose satanic figure" and a "second Lucifer."[26]

But the character of Don Alvaro is only one of several Romantic aspects of the play. Aside from presenting a typically
Romantic hero, Rivas saw to it that his work also fitted into
the Romantic mold in other respects. Let us note the violent
death of most of the important characters, including the suicide
of the hero, something which was bound to shock the more
staid theatergoers in Spain. Let us also consider the non-
observance here of the famous unities. According to Neoclassic
precepts a play should follow the unity of time (the action
should take twenty-four hours), the unity of place (the action
should take place in one location), and the unity of action
(there should be but one central action). Rivas clearly observed neither the unity of time nor that of place: years pass
between the beginning and the end, and there is a constant
change of place. Even the unity of action, which some of the
great Romantics wanted to keep for the sake of the structure
of the play,[27] is not entirely clear here. Is the central action
the tragic love of Don Alvaro and Doña Leonor, or is it the
thirst for vengeance of the Calatravas? And what about the
mystery of Don Alvaro's origin? As we have seen, at least one
critic considers it the key to the whole play. Rather than presenting us with a unity of action, has Rivas given us a unity
of interest, which a number of Romantics advocated as a sub-
stitute for the unity of action? One might say that there is unity
of interest in the sense that we are interested primarily in what
happens to the love quest of Don Alvaro. But again, there is a
shifting of interest from the problem of Don Alvaro-Doña Leonor
to the problem of Don Alvaro-the brothers Calatrava. And last
but not least, there is our interest in Don Alvaro's family problem
and its possible solutions. Thus even the unity of interest is
dubious.

In his famous *Préface du 'Cromwell,'* Victor Hugo, emphasizing
the importance of contrast in literature, wrote that modern
literature will realize that in creation "the ugly exists side by
side with the beautiful, the deformed next to the graceful, the
grotesque as the reverse of the sublime, the good with the

evil, the shadow with light."[28] These remarks can certainly
be applied to *Don Alvaro*. There are the wretched poor receiving
their food from Melitón in the last act, and next to them we
see the saintly Prior. We have the pious Padre Rafael (ex-Don
Alvaro) face to face with Don Alfonso, thirsting for revenge;
the moral ugliness of officers who cheat at cards and shortly
afterward the courage shown in battle by Spanish soldiers; the
tragic figure of Doña Leonor leaving an inn inhabited by such
down-to-earth characters as Tío (Uncle) Trabuco, the innkeeper,
and his wife; the slightly ridiculous Brother Melitón on the
one hand and the Prior and Don Alvaro on the other; the tragic
last scene of Act I, when the Marquis dies, followed by the
realistic episode in the inn, which is written in the best vein
of Spanish *costumbrismo*.[29] Among all the tragic scenes there
is the comic relief provided by the dialogue between the student
and Tío Trabuco in Act II, scene 1, and by the words of
Brother Melitón. Finally, the play, in opposition to Neoclassic
tradition, has a large number of characters, mixes verse and
prose, and uses great metrical variety. We pass from the octosyllabic *redondilla* (four eight-syllable lines rhyming *abba*), to
the *verso de romance* (eight-syllable lines in which the even-
numbered lines correspond through assonance), to the *silva*
(combination of hendecasyllables and heptasyllables), etc.

In his study of Rivas, Azorín (José Martínez Ruiz), the great
writer and critic of the Generation of '98, asserts that Rivas'
play is a "logical, natural continuation of the drama of Calderón
and Lope."[30] Other critics, too, have pointed to some echoes
of the theater of the seventeenth century in *Don Alvaro*. To
mention but a few of these elements, there is the presence of
the tragic and the comic, the metrical variety, the great number
of characters. We also have Doña Leonor's decision to lead
the life of a hermit, which echoes the traditional decisions of
many of the heroines of the Spanish Baroque drama to devote
the rest of their lives to the Lord after an unfortunate love affair.

The theme of family honor, one of the motivating forces
behind the attitude of the two brothers Calatrava (the other
being revenge), which runs through the play, recalls the many
Golden Age dramas in which honor plays such an important
role. Don Carlos says for instance: "I have come to Italy

solely / To look for the murderer / Of my father and my
honor" (p. 339) and "I have come to Italy to cleanse my
stained honor" (p. 339); Don Alfonso says: "You left my only
sister / Ruined and without honor (p. 358) and "Receive the
reward for your dishonor" (p. 363) to his sister when he
stabs her.

And last but not least, there is the soliloquy of Don Alvaro
in Act III, scene 3, where he complains of fate, which is unjust
in not allowing him to find death. This passage clearly recalls
the famous monologue of Segismundo, the hero of Calderón's
La vida es sueño (*Life Is a Dream*), Act I, scene 2, in which
Segismundo complains of his, and by extension of humanity's,
lack of freedom. The metrical form of the soliloquies is the
same: It is the *décima*, a stanza of ten octosyllabic lines rhyming
abbaaccddc, which Lope de Vega recommended for plaintive
passages. Don Alvaro says in the first *décima*, which sets the
tone for the rest:

¡Qué carga tan insufrible	What an insufferable burden
es el ambiente vital	Life is
para el mezquino mortal	For the puny mortal
que nace en signo terrible!	Who is born under a terrible sign!
¡Qué eternidad tan horrible	What a horrible eternity
la breve vida! Este mundo,	Is this short life! This world,
qué calabozo profundo	What a deep dungeon
para el hombre desdichado,	For the unfortunate man,
a quien mira el cielo airado	At whom the Heavens look
con su ceño furibundo.	With their furious frown.

(p. 331)

However, not too much should be made of the apparent
parallels with the Baroque drama. Doña Leonor, unlike the
heroines of many Golden Age plays, who are wont to enter
a convent immediately after their misfortune, and who seem
to accept their fate without questioning, almost with a matter-
of-fact attitude, waits a whole year, while she is living with
her aunt in Cordova, before she makes her decision. Only after
a long period of meditation and inner conflict does she resolve
to end her days in a remote place. The accent here, then, is

on inner motivation rather than on automatic acceptance of the dictates of society, which is the case in the Baroque drama.

The theme of family honor certainly occupies an important place in the structure of *Don Alvaro*, but here it is more than the motivating force which was part of the value system of Baroque society; rather, honor is used as an element that emphasizes the power of fate in its pursuit of Don Alvaro. Honor, together with the desire for vengeance, thus becomes the right hand of fate.

As for the famous *décimas* in Rivas and Calderón, Joaquín Casalduero has clearly analyzed the essential differences between the two passages: Don Alvaro's *décimas* are a complaint which focuses on his own, individual fate. He says for instance: "And I, who am unhappy;/ I, who am looking for it [death], / I cannot find it" (p. 331). And he gives vent to his own feeling of nostalgia with the exclamation: "Seville! Guadalquivir! / How you torment my mind" (p. 332). Segismundo in *La vida es sueño* on the other hand "faces a problem—why does he have less freedom?—; his 'I' is Man in general and he compares himself with 'the others'—birds, beasts, fish, stream—in order to elucidate the enigma of human freedom within the whole universe."[31]

As a full-blown Romantic play *Don Alvaro* relies rather heavily on coincidence, and there are a number of rather unlikely situations. Rivas has been severely taken to task on these points by Azorín. The critic argues for instance that if the clergyman had not been at the water stall in Act I, scene 2, Don Alvaro might have been able to elope with Doña Leonor.[32] He asks: "And if the pistol had not gone off? And if the bullet had not struck the marquis?"[33] And Azorín goes through the play with a fine toothcomb and digs up all the situations which he finds unlikely and absurd. But we might answer: What play has no coincidences, what play is entirely free from unlikely situations? As a matter of fact some of the coincidences in *Don Alvaro* are not at all as outrageous as Azorín claims they are. Pistols do go off accidentally on occasion. If it had not been the clergyman, it might very well have been somebody else who could have warned the Marquis. Tragedy and especially drama have "always admitted the element of chance as one of the forces which produce the catastrophe."[34] Finally Azorín forgets that

Rivas placed much emphasis on the factor of fate in this play and that all these coincidences and implausible situations are merely the workings of fate. "They are arbitrary blows of cosmic injustice falling on the hero."[35]

IV *The Power of Fate*

Rivas added a subtitle to *Don Alvaro* in order to emphasize the importance of the factor of fate in this play. The question is: Do we deal here with the fate of the Classic tragedy, this mysterious, external force which pursues inexorably the hero or heroine, or do we merely have a series of events which, though appearing as fortuitous, illustrate the power of Divine Providence? In other words, do we have a pagan or a Christian view of the life of Don Alvaro?

Critics have debated this problem ever since the first time the play was performed. Nicomedes Pastor Díaz wrote in his biography of Rivas: "The object of the drama of the Duke of Rivas is the same as that of old Greek tragedy, Destiny. Don Alvaro is an Oedipus destined by Heaven to cause the misfortune of a family, as the Greek Oedipus that of his."[36] Ferrer del Río declared flatly in 1846: "Its principal dramatic motivating force is Greek fatalism."[37] Charles de Mazade, writing at the same time, saw Don Alvaro as a man "condemned in his cradle," dragged down "from disillusion to disillusion, from grief to grief, from fall to fall till a lamentable end."[38] Blanco García in his *La literatura española en el siglo XIX* (*Spanish Literature in the 19th Century*) also saw fate as a vital ingredient of the work but stated that it is a fate different from the pagan variety and approaches that of the chance of popular beliefs.[39] Menéndez Pelayo said rather vaguely of the play that "not a Greek but a Spanish fatality is the god which guides that machine."[40] The French critic Ernest Mérimée declared in his history of Spanish literature (1908) that "the principal character is Fate, the Romantic Ananké."[41]

But there were dissenting voices. Conservative critics, dissatisfied with the above interpretations and stressing Catholic orthodoxy, insisted upon a Providentialist explanation. According to them, the dealings of Providence are manifested throughout

the play. Don Alvaro commits a crime when he tries to abduct
Doña Leonor and marry her against the wishes of her father;
he is thereafter punished by Providence, which is helped by
a series of fortuitous events. This was the position of Leopoldo
Augusto de Cueto, who said in 1866:

The violent death of her father, that of the brothers of Leonor, and
that of Leonor herself emanate more or less immediately from the
conduct of Don Alvaro, and if chance contributes to form that chain
of bloody events, it does so only to help the avenging hand of
Providence.[42]

He adds that the expiation of Don Alvaro is a "tremendous
lesson of Christian morality." This is also substantially the
view of Manuel Cañete who, objecting to the phrase "Christian
Oedipus," that a number of critics had used to describe Don
Alvaro, wrote that he saw in the play an aspect of Providential
justice. Don Alvaro made an erroneous choice when he tried
to elope with Doña Leonor, and "the Duke of Rivas does not
abandon his hero to the horrors of a criminal predestination,
inevitable like that of Oedipus, but condemns him to experiment
the consequences of the fatalism of voluntary error."[43] The same
position was taken by Enrique Funes, who wrote that the characters in *Don Alvaro* are punished by Providence.[44]

Though it appears to have some merit at first sight, this
second thesis does not really stand analysis. In the first place,
it overlooks the fact that the author himself called his play
Don Alvaro o la fuerza del sino. Therefore, Rivas intended to
show the power of something outside Don Alvaro's control,
which seemingly pursues him from beginning to end, and which
the author called "destiny." In the second place, as Blanco
García notes, if we accept the Providentialist theory, then we
must accept the fact that God punishes the crimes of one
individual with the destruction of the family whose honor he
had tried to besmirch, which would be patently absurd.[45] Finally,
we must not forget that Don Alvaro, before he committed the
faux pas of attempting to elope with Doña Leonor, in other
words before the moment when Providence would come into
the picture by arranging for punishment, was already a man

marked by an inclement fate. His parents had been jailed, he himself had been born in jail, and he had been brought up by savages, and hence his school had been the wilderness. When the gypsy girl Preciosilla speaks of Don Alvaro in Act I, scene 2, she mentions the lines of his hand and says that an evil fate awaits him. Thus, at least before the attempt at elopement, there had been something unfair about his fate and he had had no control over it.

If we do not accept the Providentialist interpretation, do we then accept the view that a fate akin to the fate of Classical tragedy pursues Don Alvaro? Closer to our days, Allison Peers grappled with the problem and came up with the answer that there are inherent contradictions in the play. Rivas had some conception of a destiny pursuing the hero, but while Don Alvaro attributes his misfortunes to destiny, "the forces set in motion by the explosion of the fatal pistol are not those of Destiny but of Free-Will, aided by coincidences which some call Providence and others chance."[46] Moreover, Rivas, while wanting to portray the force of destiny, "could not reconcile this thesis with his instinctive Christian beliefs."[47] Therefore he was deflected from his original intention, and the impression produced does not match Rivas' intention.

In a recent article, Richard A. Cardwell argues that the reason why critics have found the subtitle an obstacle in understanding the play is that there "is a general assumption that the play is realistic rather than symbolic."[48] For Cardwell, Don Alvaro is an archetype who voices the misgivings of an influential minority of the age "concerning traditional interpretations of the universe and man's status and role within it."[49] The confrontation between Don Alvaro and the members of the Calatrava family represents the clash between a new interpretation of the universe on the part of a nonconformist and the traditional and orthodox Catholic *Weltanschauung*. Don Alvaro believes that he is the victim of divine injustice and succumbs to its repeated blows.

We can certainly agree with Peers and Cardwell that the idea of destiny loomed large in the mind of Rivas at the time of the composition of *Don Alvaro*. It is a fact, as we have seen before, that from his earliest days Rivas had been preoccupied with the idea of fate. We find it in his early poetic compositions and we find it in *El paso honroso* and in *Florinda*. In *El moro expósito*, too, there are numerous references to destiny and the stars, although at the same time there is an indication throughout the poem that Providence is at work.

When Rivas began to write *Don Alvaro* in France, his own interest in the element of destiny was certainly reinforced by the ideas he had been absorbing for some time through his contacts with European Romanticism. The idea of fate is precisely one of the important conceptions of the Romantic movement. Destiny is a factor in the lives of the great Romantic heroes and the terms fate and destiny are constantly uttered by these characters. Thus Rivas decided that the hero of his new play, too, would be the victim of fate.

At the same time it is entirely possible that Rivas was identifying to some extent with Don Alvaro. He himself "seemed to be undergoing some kind of crisis of belief in the religious dogmas in which he had been educated and to be questioning many of the habitual preconceptions, values, and beliefs which were held to be essential to the safety and stability of society and that make for a harmonious view of existence."[50] Rivas had been an exile since 1823 because of the triumph of absolutism in Spain, which was strongly supported by the Church. He had come into contact with French liberalism, and his constant companion in France was the liberal Alcalá Galiano. The anticlericalism we noted in *El moro expósito* may very well have been an expression of the ideological crisis through which he was passing. He may have been viewing himself as the victim of an inclement fate, kept far from his beloved Andalusia in a country where he was living through difficult days.[51] *Don Alvaro*, then, is very possibly to a certain extent a product of Rivas' reaction to the blows of adversity. The passage which particularly points to this is Don Alvaro's exclamation in his soliloquy: "Seville! Guadalquivir! / How you torment my mind" (p. 332).

However, in spite of the religious doubts which were troubling him, Rivas could not shed his instinctive Christian beliefs. Throughout much of the play the atmosphere is religious. Aside from the fact that Doña Leonor and her brothers are good

Catholics, Don Alvaro himself conforms to religious standards: When he plans to elope with Doña Leonor, he also plans to marry her in a religious ceremony. A number of times he uses conventional phrases involving God.[52] At the moment when he is saved from execution by the Austrian attack at the end of Act IV he makes a vow to God to renounce the world if he is not killed in battle, and he keeps his promise by entering the Franciscan monastery. When he wounds Don Alfonso he tells him: "Ask God for forgiveness" (p. 362). Only at the very end does Don Alvaro break with religious orthodoxy by uttering blasphemies and by committing suicide. But even then the chorus of friars asking God for mercy is a religious manifestation.

It is mainly because of this religious factor that we cannot agree with the interpretation of Cardwell concerning the symbolic nature of the play. Whatever Rivas' intention, and in spite of the ending, Don Alvaro is not *the* Romantic rebel who symbolizes man's loss of hope in a well-ordered universe. While Don Alvaro sees himself as the victim of cosmic injustice, he is at the same time too orthodox to rise to the heights of a Romantic archetype expressing Romantic unhappiness with society and the cosmos. Actually Don Alvaro can be said to rebel only twice against the order of things: When he attempts to elope with Doña Leonor, and when he commits suicide. This last act is, of course, a gesture of supreme rebellion—especially for a Catholic, but it takes place at the end of the play, when Don Alvaro has lost all hope in cosmic justice. Otherwise, as stated above, he is essentially a conformist. A further example of this conformity is the scene in Act IV in which the captain suggests that the army might rise to free Don Alvaro. The latter indignantly rejects this possibility: "The army could / Fail in its discipline, / And I would owe my head / To a rebellion? . . . No, never" (p. 350).

To sum up then: Following his own penchant already expressed in previous works, and as a good disciple of Romanticism, Rivas decided to portray the force of destiny and brought out this aspect in a number of ways in the play. Don Alvaro is born into a family with serious problems; the lines on his hand announce an evil fate; he himself believes that he is the victim of an inclement destiny, and in the case of the brothers Cala-trava the factors of honor and revenge act as irresistible forces which drive the two men and Don Alvaro to perdition. Actually honor and the thirst for vengeance are the play's most potent expressions of fate. It is true that Don Alvaro chooses of his free will to defy the Marquis' wishes; but after the accident with the pistol, the rest of the play, given the power of honor and revenge, is an inevitable and irresistible succession of events.

What we have then, as Peers has noted, is a basic contra-diction, though not because the forces set in motion are those of free will. There is on the one hand the religious atmosphere of the play—the references to God; but on the other hand God's will is not really apparent. It is as if He had decided not to intervene through Providence and to let fate run its course. Rivas was orthodox enough to point to the existence of God and to make his characters God-fearing, but he strongly em-phasized the factor of destiny and did not let God interfere with its actions. There is then an essential contradiction between the pagan and the Christian aspects of *Don Alvaro*; but if Rivas realized that the end result of his play was contradictory, he was apparently happy to let the work stand or fall with it.

CHAPTER 5

Rivas' "Nationalized" Romanticism: The Romances históricos

I Rivas and the Spanish Ballad

IN 1841, Rivas published the *Romances históricos* (*Historical Ballads*) which, everything considered, must be regarded as his most attractive work and his most important contribution to Spanish Romanticism. They were written between 1830 and 1840 and some of them, such as "El Conde de Villamediana" ("Count Villamediana") and "El alcázar de Sevilla" ("The Palace of Seville") appeared as early as 1834, together with *Florinda*, in the first edition of *El moro expósito*.

In most of the *Romances históricos* the poet deals with either well-documented historical incidents or with anecdotes which popular tradition had etched over the ages into Spanish national consciousness. We go from the fourteenth century and the sinister figure of King Pedro the Cruel to the fifteenth century and the death of the royal favorite Don Alvaro de Luna, to some of the tribulations of Columbus, to the youthful Hernán Cortés, the Spanish victories over the French in Italy during the reign of Charles V, thence to an evil deed of Philip II, on to the death of Count Villamediana at the beginning of the reign of Philip IV in the seventeenth century, to the Spanish victory at Bailén over the Napoleonic troops in 1808. Three of the *romances* (ballads), "El cuento de un veterano" ("A Veteran's Tale"), "La vuelta deseada" ("The Longed-for Return"), and "El sombrero" ("The Hat") are pure fiction, although in at least one of them, "El cuento de un veterano," we are given a specific historical background, the War of the Austrian Succession in Italy in the 1740's.

There are eighteen stories or incidents in all, all but one of which[1] are divided into various *romances*. Thus "Una antigualla de Sevilla" ("An Old Tale of Seville") is divided into three *romances* entitled "El candil" ("The Oil Lamp"), "El juez" ("The Judge"), and "La cabeza" ('The Head"). Each *romance* is written in the traditional ballad meter, i.e., eight-syllable lines, with the odd verses blank and the even ones in assonance.[2] The lines are grouped into quatrains. When a new subdivision of the poem begins there is a change in assonance.

With the *Romances históricos* Rivas gave new life to a poetic genre which is one of Spain's great contributions to world literature. Spain's popular genius shone more than anywhere else in her ballads, the *romances*, these narrative, often lyrical, poems which are thought to have made their appearance in the fifteenth century, perhaps as early as the late fourteenth century.[3] The epic features of the early ballads and their austere tone led a number of critics to believe that they were fragments of the old epic poems which, while recited in their entirety by *juglares* or bards in the castles, were too long to be recited in their entirety in the market place. According to this theory, which is widely accepted today,[4] the *juglares* would eventually tell their town public only the most striking fragments of epic poems, and thus these fragments or *romances* would become the patrimony of the people. These old *romances* dealt with historical and legendary themes, such as the story of King Roderick, the seven Infantes of Lara, the Cid, etc.[5] *Romances* not connected with the old epic poems were later written on many other themes, and in the sixteenth and seventeenth centuries recognized poets wrote *romances*, often injecting lyrical elements into the narrative structure of the ballad or writing in a completely lyrical vein. The *romances* lost some of their popularity in the eighteenth century, although a number of poets continued to write them,[6] but European Romanticism, attracted by primitive poetry and the popular spirit found in it, gave the *romance* its unstinted admiration, especially in Germany and England.[7] In Spain, too, Romanticism brought about a revival of the *romance*, and in this revival Rivas played a paramount role.[8]

Rivas has left very little in the way of observations on his own work, but he did pen a fairly lengthy prologue to the first

edition of his *Romances históricos.* In it he gives vent to his
enthusiasm for the Spanish ballad meter and writes:

The *romance,* the national meter of our language, in which were
sung the deeds of our forefathers, which was cultivated and adorned
by our best poets, which so pleases the ear in theatrical dialogue,
which so easily adapts itself to all subjects, to all styles, so simple,
so sonorous, abode of the assonant, exclusive beauty of our beautiful
language . . . must not be scorned nor forgotten on account of meters
and rhythmic combinations which we have taken, to great advantage, it is true, from another language.[9] And although with them
our own language has become richer and many admirable works have
been written . . . , let us not give up the rich treasure of Castilian
poetic elocution which we possess in the octosyllabic *romances* nor
lay aside one of our best titles to poetic glory.[10]

Aside from expressing his admiration for the ballad and the
ballad meter Rivas gives the reader a short history of the *romance* but in the process commits several errors. He claims for
instance that the *romance* constitutes the oldest Spanish popular poetry, whereas chronologically the *cantares de gesta* (epic
poems), like the *Poema del Cid,* with their irregular versifica-
tion, came first. He also asserts that the material found in the
romances was used for the composition of the *crónicas* or his-
tories written in prose at a later date. It is recognized today that
much material preserved in prose form in the *crónicas* derives
not from the *romances* but from the primitive *cantares de gesta.*[11]
   In the same prologue Rivas also states that in his own day,
when poets looked for medieval themes, no other meter was
more appropriate to this purpose than the eight-syllable *romance,* "since it was born in the period of the heroes who are
now extolled" (pp. 395–96). The *romance octosílabo* is also the
most appropriate meter for the "daring, varied, and unequal
flights of Romanticism" (p. 396). Rivas' purpose in writing the
Historical Ballads is clearly stated in the concluding paragraph
of the prologue:

The *romance,* then, so well-suited . . . for narration and description,
to express philosophical thoughts and for dialogue, must above all
triumph in historical poetry, in the telling of memorable events;

in this manner it started out in the hard centuries of its birth. Returning it to its original aim and to its primitive vigor and energetic simplicity, without forgetting the progress of language, of the taste for philosophy, and taking advantage of all the finery with which our great writers have adorned it, would be a task for the outstanding poets, who are never absent from our privileged land. With limited strength I have endeavored to carry out such a difficult and important undertaking in writing this collection of historical ballads which I present to the public. (p. 401)

II *Nationalism in the* Romances históricos

A contemporary of Rivas, the poet and critic Enrique Gil y Carrasco, reviewing the *Romances históricos* in *El Pensamiento* in 1841, wrote: "There are in these *romances* so many things to flatter our pride, please our memory, and arouse our feeling of nationality, that their impression cannot fail to be highly noble and patriotic."[12] Nationalism is indeed one of the features of a good proportion of the *Historical Ballads*. In these poems we have none of the Byronic poses of an Espronceda nor the metaphysical despair of a Larra. Rivas, always a patriot, has become more and more nationalistic in the decade of the 1830's. His interest and pride in Spanish history is intense. Thus what we have in some of the *romances* is a recreation of some striking and macabre events of Spanish history and in others an unabashed glorification of Spain's great historical moments—or at least what many Spaniards considered to be great historical moments—told in superb verse replete with brilliant descriptions and a national pride that fairly vibrates throughout much of this work.

In "Recuerdos de un grande hombre" ("Recollections of a Great Man"), composed in Gibraltar in 1837, which recounts the tribulations of Christopher Columbus and owes much to Washington Irving's *The Life and Voyages of Columbus*,[13] there is a quatrain which pays homage to the Catholic Monarchs in the following terms: "The Two Catholic Monarchs / Who are Spain's Atlantes, / Who founded an empire / Which no empire equals."[14] We have particularly lavish praise of Queen Isabella the Catholic, who for so many Spaniards throughout the ages has incarnated Castilian virtues and Castilian determination.

Isabella is described at the moment when she gives her jewels to Columbus to finance his voyage. The poet gives an epic tone to his description:

> Her heroic soul, blazing
> With enthusiasm and powerful faith,
> Source of great acts,
> Her noble breast filled with resolution,
>
> She takes off her high diadem
> And from her breast she takes
> The rich insignia
> Of incalculable value. (p. 346)

For Rivas, as for so many other conservative Spaniards (by 1837 Rivas had become quite conservative), patriotism went hand in hand with religious faith, and this factor was present here, when Isabella, addressing Columbus, says:

Lleva a ese ignorado mundo
los castellanos pendones
con la santa fe de Cristo,
con la gloria de mi nombre.

El Cielo tu rumbo guíe,
y cuando glorioso tornes . . .

tu hazaña bendiga el Cielo,
to arrojo el infierno asombre.

Take to that unknown world
The Castilian standards
With the holy faith of Christ,
With the glory of my name.

May Heaven guide your path,
And when you return bedecked
  with glory . . .

May Heaven bless your deed,
May your boldness astonish hell.
(p. 346)

Unabashed nationalism is the hallmark of the series of *romances* which tell of the confrontation between Spain and France at the end of the fifteenth century and the beginning of the sixteenth. In "Un embajador español" ("A Spanish Ambassador")[15] King Charles VIII of France, who has invaded Italy, is ravaging the papal states. The Spanish ambassador Don Antonio de Fonseca, representing his king, ally of the Pope, reminds the French monarch of his treaty with France by which he had guaranteed to respect the interests of Castile and of the

Papacy. Fonseca reads the treaty to him, and as Charles VIII
cynically erases the clauses which favor Castile and the Papacy,
the Spanish envoy tears up the paper on which the treaty is
written and throws the pieces at the feet of the French king.

This poem is a vivid example of how vowel stress can de-
termine the tone of a poetic passage. The first of the two *romances* comprising "Un embajador español," relates how Charles
VIII cannot be moved from his nefarious course in spite of all
entreaties, using even-numbered lines with assonance in *aa*. The
second *romance,* which deals with the Spanish ambassador, consists of foreshortened, seven-syllable *octosílabos,* with assonance
in *e.* These *agudo* (sharp) endings express perfectly the firmness
and pride with which Don Antonio de Fonseca faces his country's rival and seem to signal the end of humiliation and the
beginning of resistance. Due to the change in assonance, the
contrast in tone between the last quatrain of the first ballad and
the first quatrain of the second is striking.

End of first *romance*:
The French king does not listen to reason.

pues con desabrido gesto	Since with rude bearing
y con burladora r*abia*[16]	And with mocking rage,
que no recuerda, responde,	He answers that he does not remember
de cuanto le dicen, n*ada*	Anything of what they tell him.

(p. 349)

Second *romance*:
The Spanish ambassador appears on the scene.

Don Antonio de Fonseca,	Don Antonio de Fonseca,
caballero de alta l*ey*,	A knight of sterling character,
de los católicos reyes	Is the noble ambassador
en noble embajador *es*.	Of the Catholic Monarchs.
Preséntase con modestia,	He introduces himself with modesty,
pero con el rostro qu*e*	But with a face whose expression
cara de pocos amigos	The common people call correctly
llama el vulgo y llama bi*en*	A tough countenance. (p. 349)

Toward the end of the poem the same assonance underscores the haughty attitude of the Spanish ambassador:

tiró los rotos pedazos	He threw the torn pieces
del rey de Francia a los pi*es*,	At the feet of the king of France
y calándose el sombrero	And putting on his hat
sin hacer venia se fu*e*	He left without bowing his head.

(p. 350)

In the ballad "Amor, honor y valor" ("Love, Honor, and Valor"), which describes the Italian campaigns of the Emperor Charles V,[17] we read the lines "The undefeated Spanish / Formations, whose glory / Is the wonder of the Universe" (p. 358). The great victory of Charles V over Francis I of France at the battle of Pavia in 1525 gave Rivas material for another *romance*, "La victoria de Pavía" ("The Victory of Pavia"), and in it his patriotism is given free rein. We read for instance, "There is no rank that is not destroyed / By the harquebuses of Spain, / There is no horse that they do not put to flight, / There is no warrior whom they do not knock down" (p. 365). At one point the Marquis of Pescara, the victor in the battle, says to Francis I of France, who has been made a prisoner: "For the Spanish nation, / Which achieves such a great triumph, / Is as noble in victory as in battle courageous" (p. 369).

Against the background of the anonymous mass of Charles V's army, Rivas incarnates Spanish valor in a few concrete individuals. One of these is the Andalusian Roldán, who hails from Seville. Roldán, like many Andalusians, has a good sense of humor. He hands King Francis I of France a bullet of gold which he had melted specially to kill the French monarch. As he gives this bullet to Francis he remarks that it could possibly contribute to his ransom. This incident, which is not the product of the poet's imagination, for it actually occurred,[18] permitted Rivas to convey to the reader something of his Andalusian patriotism. Rivas' intense nationalism most probably owes something to the Spanish War of Independence against Napoleon (1808–14), in which he himself took an active part. That there was some residue of Francophobia in the Duke cannot be doubted; it certainly emerges at the end of this poem. As Rivas

recalls the shameful moment when he had been obliged to escort
the sword of Francis I to the headquarters of Joachim Murat,
Napoleon's lieutenant in Spain, in 1808, he exclaims, alluding to
the victory of Bailén over the French: "And instead of this
jewel, Spain / Was able to add by God / To the great name of
Pavia / That of Bailén, which is greater" (p. 372).

One of the most attractive *romances* of the series is the
one entitled "Un castellano leal" ("A Loyal Castilian").[19] In it
Count Benavente, ordered by Charles V to give lodging in his
palace to the Duke of Borbón, a Frenchman who had turned
against his master Francis I and joined Charles V, burns down
his abode to purify it of the presence of a traitor. Count Benavente is the incarnation of Castilian pride and nobility. At the
beginning of the poem he expresses himself thus: "If he is a
cousin of kings, / I am a cousin of kings; / And I am Count of
Benavente, / If he is Duke of Borbón. / I have an advantage
over him, / In that my noble blood / Has never been stained by
treason / And by virtue of the fact that I was born a Spaniard"
(p. 372).

The *romance* in which Rivas' patriotism is strongest is "Bailén,"
which recounts the great Spanish victory over Napoleon's army
at Bailén in northern Andalusia in July, 1808. Bailén was one of
the most crucial military events of the War of Independence.
After the French defeat at Bailén, Napoleon was forced to
commit hundreds of thousands of men to the Peninsula; Spain
became a cancer in the body of the French Empire and deci-
sively contributed to its end. Written in 1839, "Bailén" fittingly
adds an important event of the nineteenth century to the historical panorama presented by the collection of historical *romances*. This time Rivas speaks not of remote ages but of something that had happened in his lifetime during a war in which
he himself had been involved.

The historical importance of the victory, the poet's own in-
volvement in the war, and the strong nationalistic feeling that the
famous battle aroused in Rivas all combine to give this *romance*
a stronger epic character than some of the other poems in the
collection. The first of the three parts, entitled "Sevilla," begins
with a glorifying evocation of Seville: "At opulent Seville, / The
city with the enchanted castle, / The city with the magnificent

temple, / The city with the proud tower; / Emporium of wealth, / Home of great minds, / And which slept in the arms / Of peace and abundance . . . (p. 413). This evocation sets the tone which Rivas will maintain throughout the composition. Even the messenger, who brings evil tidings to Seville, is out of the ordinary: "His face as if made of brimstone, / His eyes as if live coals, / Prove that he is a messenger / Of dangers and misfortunes" (p. 413).

At the news of the French advance on Andalusia, all Seville awakens to the danger, and, as one man, prepares for war. Accumulation and anaphoras, bunched together in relatively few stanzas, play a major role here in conveying the awe-inspiring war effort of the great city:

No hay ya opuestos intereses,	There are no longer conflicting interests,
No hay ya clases encontradas,	There are no longer conflicting classes,
No hay ya distintos deseos,	There are no longer different desires,
No hay ya opiniones contrarias,	There are no longer clashing opinions,
Ni más pasión que la ira,	Nor is there any other passion but anger,
Ni más amor que la patria,	Nor any other love but the fatherland,
Ni más anhelo que guerra,	Nor any other longing but war,
Ni más grito que "¡venganza!"	Nor any other cry but "Vengeance!"
Palacios, talleres, templos,	Palaces, shops, temples,
conventos, humildes casas,	Monasteries, humble houses,
academias, tribunales,	Academies, tribunals,
lonjas, oficinas, aulas,	Exchanges, offices, classrooms,
tórnanse en cuartel inmenso,	Are turned into an immense armed camp,
donde sólo crujen armas,	Where only weapons clang,
sólo retumban tambores,	Where only drums resound,
sólo se alistan escuadras.	Where only squads are formed.

(p. 413)

The shouts of "guerra y muerte" (war and death) and "¡Vamos a matar franceses!" (Let us kill Frenchmen!) resound throughout the city, and the first part ends with a personification of the great landmark of Seville, the tower called the Giralda. The huge tower stands out against the sky, tolling its bells and calling on all Andalusia and all Spain to make war. Particularly felicitous is the metaphor used in describing the bonfire which tops the Giralda: "And it adorns its upright forehead, / As dark night falls, / With a crown of bonfires, / Which are not put out by wind and rain; / It is the flag of the holy fire / Which has been lit at its feet, / The crater of the tremendous volcano, / Which explodes in that great Seville" (p. 414).

The second part, entitled "La agresión" ("Aggression"), deals with Napoleon and his campaign against Spain. There is a certain ambivalence in Rivas' attitude toward Napoleon, an ambivalence also seen in other Spanish Romantics.[20] The Emperor is shown as the cruel enemy of Spain, but at the same time Rivas recognizes that Napoleon is a gigantic, willful figure, a "prodigious combination of angel, man, and devil," who obviously inspires some measure of grudging admiration in the poet. But whatever good there had been in this epic figure, it disappeared when he cast his greedy eye on Spain, and the memory of Napoleon's actions with respect to the Spanish royal family and the people of Madrid evokes harsh words from the poet.

After the second part Rivas proceeds to sing the victory at Bailén in the third and last part, "La victoria." It begins on a highly lyric note.[21] The first two quatrains read as follows:

> Bailén! . . . Oh magic name!
> What Spaniard on pronouncing it
> Does not feel burning in his chest
> The volcano of enthusiasm?
>
> Bailén; . . . The purest glory
> Which History sees in its annals
> And which the present century admires,
> Established its throne in your fields. (p. 415)

The tone of this passage recalls the style of the traditional patriotic ode and that of a composition to the victory of Bailén

written by Rivas in his youth. Toward the end of this latter poem
entitled "To the Victory of Bailén," Rivas had written in 1808:

> Yours is the triumph, Spain, my fatherland,
> And the sacred laurel belongs to your sons.
> Your courage and your just ire
> Triumphed, and no longer is it possible
> For the Frenchman to resist, the Frenchman who, downhearted,
> Wets his cheek with wet tears
> And, humbled, casts down the useless sword. (p. 21)

In the later work, the two armies are on a collision course—
the Spaniards without experience in war but with God and
justice on their side, against the fierce French veterans. God
decides that Spanish faith and valor "shall stop the colossus"[22];
Spanish arms are victorious, and the French surrender.

The epic poem normally requires the presence of a hero.
That part is nominally played here by General Castaños, Duke
of Bailén, to whom the composition is dedicated. However, his
role is a very small one, as he is mentioned only twice in the
course of the whole poem. Actually, Castaños, in command of
the Spanish armies in Andalusia, had not been present at the
crucial moment of the battle. Moreover, what Rivas wanted to
emphasize, and what so many writers have emphasized when
dealing with the war, was the part played by the inexperienced
Spanish army that had fought at Bailén: "And in defeat the
legions / Which humiliated the universe, / March by in chains, /
Their glory turned into mockery, / Before a mob which two
months ago / Busy in shop and with plow / Could not even
load a rifle" (p. 417).

At the end Rivas introduces the supernatural element, so
often used in epic compositions, but absent in almost all the
other *romances históricos*: "From the throne of God / Two
archangels flew: / One, to take the news to the pole / Turning
its snow into fire; / The other, to dig a tomb / On St. Helena,
a rock / Which down there in the torrid zone / Stands out in the
Ocean" (p. 417).

III   *Macabre Elements*

Aside from the nationalism found in this collection and the
general fascination with the national past, both of which are

Romantic ingredients, we should note another Romantic characteristic, the macabre, which we meet in quite a few *romances.*
Typical in this respect are the three poems devoted to Pedro
the Cruel (1334–69), the fourteenth-century king of Castile,
who has been portrayed by Spaniards throughout the ages alter-
nately as a beast of prey and as a *rey justiciero* (a just and fair
king). Rivas takes away nothing of his cruelty, yet at the same
time gives him the almost epic aspect of a figure before whom
we must stand in awe. In "The Oil Lamp," the first of the three
romances forming the ballad "Una antigualla de Sevilla" ("An
Old Tale of Seville"),[23] a poor old woman witnesses the death
of a man in a duel below her window. The tone of the poem
is set by this lugubrious event and by the repulsive aspect of
the woman, whose arms and hands are nothing but skin and
bones, and whose face is that of a "frightful witch." The old
woman realizes that the killer is King Pedro himself when she
hears the characteristic cracking noise made by his kneecaps as
he walks away from the scene of the duel. Needless to say, she
is terrified, and her fear causes her to drop an oil lamp to the
street.

The action of "El juez" ("The Judge"), the next part of "Una
antigualla de Sevilla," takes place in the palace of the King,
where the latter, playing the role of *justiciero* (a just monarch),
demands of the mayor of the town that he produce the same
night the head of the person guilty of the crime. The dialogue
with the mayor, Martín Fernández Cerón, is crisp and shows
Pedro as an inflexible despot. Dramatic scenes like this are found
quite often in the *Romances históricos* and give these poems a
certain dramatic quality which is one of their charms.[24]

Contrast, too, is used to good effect in this part of "An Old
Tale of Seville." On the one hand the poet underlines the dark
side of the King's character, after the Mayor exits, by pointing
to his "sinister" eyes and the "satanic" laughter that one notes
in them, and on the other his peaceful activities in the course
of the rest of the day as he visits the ships anchored in the
Guadalquivir, prays in the church of Santa Ana, plays checkers
with Martín Gil de Albuquerque, and goes riding.

But in the third part, "La cabeza" ("The Head"), we are
plunged once again into a sinister atmosphere as Mayor Cerón

is ready to hear the depositions of a witness to the crime, in a vault of the jail of Seville. The horrible vault, the presence of two executioners, and the lugubrious assonance in *u-a* combine to make this a most gloomy scene. Its first quatrains set the tone:

Al tiempo que en el ocaso	At the time when in the West
Su eterna llama sep*u*lt*a*	The sun buries its eternal flame,
el sol, y tierra y cielos	And when earth and sky
con negras sombras se enl*u*t*a*n,	Dress in mourning with dark shadows,
de la cárcel de Sevilla,	In a dark vault
en una bóveda osc*u*r*a*,	Of the jail of Seville,
que una lámpara de cobre	Which a copper lamp
más bien asombra que al*u*mbr*a*,	Darkens rather than lights,
pasaba una extraña escena	There took place a strange scene,
de aquellas que nos ang*u*sti*a*n,	One of those which causes us anguish,
si en horrenda pesadilla	When in a horrible nightmare
el sueño nos las dib*u*j*a*.	Sleep draws them for us.
Pues no asemejaba cosa	For it did not seem a thing
de este mundo, aunque se *u*s*a*n	Of this world, although we find in it
en él cosas harto horrendas	Rather horrible things
de que he presenciado	Of which I have witnessed
m*u*ch*a*s. . . .	many. . . . (p. 315)

The witness is brought in. It is none other than the unfortunate old woman who had seen the duel from her window. Dreading the King's ire she refuses to identify the killer and as a result is tortured. With somber realism the poet tells us how the bones in her hand crack as unbearable pressure is applied through an "apparatus of iron." Unable to bear the pain she cries out that it was the King himself. It so happens that the latter had been hiding all this time behind a pillar witnessing the torture scene. Now he steps forward, and in a generous mood he gives the old woman a hundred old coins, for she has told the truth. "Yes, I am the one who killed the man," he says, "but only God judges me" (p. 317). However, in order that justice may be

done, the head of the criminal, in the form of a bust of the
King, is placed in a niche of the street where the killing had
taken place. Thus, something of the tradition of the *justiciero*
king is kept in this *romance* of the cycle of Peter the Cruel.

But there is nothing fair or just about the king portrayed
in the *romance* "El alcázar de Sevilla" ("The Palace of Seville").[25]
Here we have before us Peter the Cruel, a beast who engages
in atrocious murders, one of which is the murder of his own
brother Don Fadrique, who has just conquered for him the
town of Jumilla from the Aragonese. But before we are plunged
into this horrible event and as a striking contrast with it, we have
a lyric introduction, a praise of the palace of Seville and its
gardens, which the poet, at the time of composition a political
refugee in France, evokes with deep nostalgia. However, in the
midst of these pleasant recollections, the poet remembers that
even when he walked in those beautiful gardens and halls he
would see the ghost of Doña María de Padilla, mistress of King
Pedro, uttering a moan as she passed before his eyes. He would
also see the ghost of the King, covered with "frozen blood," and
a corpse in the entrance hall: "Even now on the flagstones one
sees / A tenacious dark stain. . . . / Not even the ages erase it! /
Blood! Blood! Oh heavens, how many / Without knowing it,
tread on it" (p. 318).

King Pedro is seen in one of the halls of the *alcázar* (palace)
of Seville in the company of María de Padilla. He is awaiting
the arrival of his brother Don Fadrique whom he suspects of
having had an affair with his wife, the Queen, Doña Blanca.
Jealousy is devouring him. In his description of the King the
poet chooses the terms which will best express the fearsome
character of the man: his glances are "sinister and terrible"; his
eyes, which are like "coals from hell," emit "fierce flames"; his
lips form a "ferocious and bitter" smile. He is compared to a
tiger and, because of the peculiar cracking noise made by his
kneecaps, to a rattlesnake.

Don Fadrique arrives, and as he sets foot in the entrance hall
of the *alcázar*, the King, "like an apparition from hell," from one
of the balconies, cries out the order to kill his brother. Again,
a grimly realistic scene is painted as six mace bearers crush
Fadrique's skull. Fadrique falls to the ground, his broken skull

"pouring out a sea of blood" (p. 322). But Rivas wants to derive the maximum macabre effect from this passage. The King is like a tiger who is aroused by the sight of blood. He pursues one of the servants of Don Fadrique to the very room of Doña María de Padilla, where the unfortunate man hopes to save himself by taking into his arms one of the little daughters of Pedro and María. He kneels before Don Pedro with the child in his arms, but to no avail. The dagger of the King pierces his heart.

The incredible personality of Don Pedro is given extraordinary plasticity, as observed in "Una antigualla de Sevilla," through contrast: "As if nothing new had occurred in the palace / The King sat down at the table / To eat as is his habit" (p. 323). After the meal he plays checkers, takes a walk, and at night goes to see his other mistress, Doña Aldonza. As he returns to the palace he sees the body of his brother on the floor of the entrance hall. Apparently he is not quite dead. Handing his sword to one of his guards Pedro says: "Finish him off, and calmly / Went upstairs and fell asleep" (p. 323). The horror of the whole *romance* is thus cleverly brought to a shocking climax.

In "El fratricidio" ("Fratricide"), we no longer witness the cruelties of King Pedro but are told of his last hours and his death at the hands of his half-brother Enrique de Trastámara.[26] Don Pedro is besieged in the castle of Montiel. Using the gloomy assonance *u-o*, which contributes to create a sinister atmosphere, the poet describes the castle in particularly lugubrious terms in the second part, the *romance* entitled "El castillo" ("The Castle"):

Era una noche de marzo,
de un marzo invernal y crudo,
en que con negras tinieblas

se viste el orbe de luto.

El castillo, cuya torre
del homenaje el oscuro
cielo taladraba altiva,
formaba de un monte el bulto.

It was a night in March,
A wintry and crude March,
In which the world dresses in
mourning
With dark shadows.

The castle, whose main tower
Pierced haughtily
The dark sky,
Formed the bulk of an eminence.
(pp. 324–25)

"The castle was surrounded / As a dead man is encircled / By yellow candles, / By bonfires auguring sad events" (p. 325). In the courtyard of the castle a fire is burning, which projects an infernal light. Satanic elements, dear to Romanticism but also very appropriate to the atmosphere of the Don Pedro cycle, are mentioned a number of times in these poems, and here, after the mention of hell, we are told of "satanic groups," which crowd around the fire and project shadows of "fantastic shapes" on the walls.

In the meantime the King has a terrible nightmare wherein his murdered victims seem to attack him; among them is Don Fadrique. "Don Fadrique," the sleeping King wails, "do not strangle me. . . . / Do not look at me, you are burning me" (p. 326). We are reminded of Shakespeare's *Richard III* in this scene, and, as Boussagol notes, it is possible that Rivas had read this play.[27] The anguish of the King is well expressed in the accumulation of substantives in the following quatrain: "Oh, I am swimming in blood! / What swords, tell me, are those? / What nooses? What poisons? / What bones? What skulls?" (p. 327).

Don Pedro, followed by his lieutenant, Men Rodríguez de Sanabria, makes his way to the tent of their enemy, the French mercenary Beltrán Claquín (Bertrand Du Guesclin), who fights in the service of Pedro's half-brother Enrique. Claquín had promised to place a lantern in front of his tent as a signal if he found that he could in some way help Pedro. The lantern had appeared and Pedro and Sanabria, putting their faith in Claquín's word, hurry to meet him. But as they enter the tent everything seems gloomy. They are surrounded by armed and silent Frenchmen whose blue eyes reflect the light of the lantern which acts like a "sinister meteor." In the next quatrain the word "sinister" is repeated: to the Spaniards everything seems to have a "sinister and grim aspect" (p. 327).

Then Claquín and Enrique enter the tent. The two half-brothers have never seen each other, and Enrique asks: "Which of these two is he?" (p. 327). Again, the adjective *satánico* is used, in this instance to describe Enrique's tone of voice. And at the end of the *romance*, after Enrique, with the help of the treacherous Claquín, has killed Don Pedro, we read: "In the camp a *viva* resounded, / And hell repeated it" (p. 328).

Why this repeated allusion to Satan and to hell? The simplest explanation is that the poet felt that the adjective *satánico* and the noun *infierno* or "hell" would effectively underscore the evil quality of the monstrous Don Pedro, of his followers, and in one instance that of Enrique. But Rivas the Romantic has also made King Pedro a Romantic villain whose character makes him akin to Lucifer. The references to hell are used to convey the grandiose power emanating from that man and his overwhelming wilfulness. Don Pedro is thus no ordinary villain. He is, as we have noted before, an epic figure whose crimes and arrogance are so great that the link to hell is the most appropriate way in which the poet can describe him. This epic quality of Don Pedro, heightened by the legend of his occasional sense of fair play, made the King almost a Spanish folk figure and was no doubt one of the reasons why Rivas devoted three series of *romances* to him.[28]

Less macabre than the cycle of Don Pedro the Cruel is the *romance* about Don Alvaro de Luna (1390–1453), the favorite of King John II of Castile (1407–54) and the power behind the Castilian throne for more than thirty years.[29] Nonetheless, the poet concentrates on the last day of Luna and describes his death at the hands of the executioner, so that the atmosphere of the bulk of the poem is definitely on the lugubrious side. When the former favorite is en route as a prisoner to Valladolid, "piensa ya ver de la muerte / la terrible sombra, en cuya / oscuridad para siempre / corre a hundirse, y se atribula." (He thinks he sees already / The terrible shadow of death / In whose darkness / He is about to sink, and he loses heart," p. 331). We note here the assonance in *u-a*, which contributes to the gloomy atmosphere of this part of the poem.

A typically Romantic incident, reminiscent of the nightmare of Don Pedro in "El fratricidio" is provided in the third part when, after arriving in Valladolid, Luna suddenly sees a specter rise in front of his mule. It is the specter of Alonso López Vivero, whom Luna had killed by throwing him out of a window. The condemned man is frightened, but he finds the strength to spend his last night as befits a "Christian, a knight, / A man of faith and of high rank" (p. 332).

The fourth *romance* of the poem describes the execution.

The condemned man mounts the scaffold and serenely faces the executioner. Calmly he exchanges some words with a few persons present. When the executioner takes out a rope to tie his hands together, Luna gives him a gold-colored ribbon and tells him to tie his hands with that instead. With marvelous concision the last quatrain relates the last horrible moment: "El hacha cae como un rayo, / salta la insigne cabeza, / se alza universal gemido / y tres campanadas suenan" ("The ax falls like a thunderbolt, / The illustrious head flies off, / A collective moan is heard / And three bell strokes resound," p. 334).

One of the grimmest endings in all the *romances* is found in "El solemne desengaño" ("The Solemn Disillusionment"), written in 1838.[30] It is the story of Francis of Borja, Marquis of Lombay, one of the most brilliant noblemen of the court of the Emperor Charles V at Toledo. In spite of his wealth and his great talents, he is a sad young man. Cleverly the narrator implies that he is desperately in love with the young empress. During a serious illness, caused no doubt by his emotional problems, the Marquis is attended by his friend, the poet Garcilaso de la Vega, who at midnight raises a tapestry which hides the opening of a secret passage. We have now a typically Romantic scene: Through the secret door a "vago bulto silencioso" (a vaguely outlined, silent form) appears, who seems to be a "supernatural product of some incantation." This person looks at the sick man with eyes that are like live coals and strokes his feverish forehead with a hand which appears to be of ice, after which the apparition leaves. Again, the poet delicately lets us draw the only logical conclusion—that this form was that of the Empress, aware of the hidden love of the nobleman and distraught by his illness.

But the young Empress dies, and Toledo is in mourning. Her body is to be transferred for burial from Toledo to the Cathedral of Granada, where lie the remains of the Catholic Monarchs Ferdinand and Isabella. The heartbroken Marquis is in the cortege accompanying the imperial coffin. When after a long journey the casket arrives in the cathedral, Lombay must identify the body. A page lifts the lid, and now the author, with pitiless realism, informs us that such a terrible stench arises from the coffin that "the lights lose their brightness." We may be surprised at first glance by such a realistic passage in a Romantic. But we must keep in mind that Realism and Romanticism are not necessarily, and not always mutually, exclusive and that Romantics, following one of the tenets of their creed (that life in all its aspects should be portrayed), often insert realistic passages into their works.[31] The marquis lifts a tissue of lace which hides the head. Horrors! The beautiful face has been turned into a stinking, shapeless mass on which a swarm of worms feed. The contrast between the evocation of the face of "roses and candid snow," of the "divine mouth of pearls and carnations,"[32] and the "eyes of fire" on the one hand and the repulsive aspect of the dead head on the other is indeed striking, and if Rivas wanted to shock the reader he certainly succeeded. But the realism of the description also has the aim of making the end appear more plausible: The Marquis is so overwhelmed by this awful spectacle that when he recovers from the blow he decides to devote the rest of his life to God. In his words, "No more shall I burn my soul / With a sun which can become extinguished / Nor shall I serve lords / Who become worms" (p. 386). Thus a new saint is born, St. Francis of Borja.

From the period of Charles V we go to the reign of Philip II (1556–98), that complex personality who has aroused so much interest over the centuries. In "Una noche de Madrid en 1578" ("A Night in Madrid in 1578"),[33] this King of Spain is depicted as a more sinister personage perhaps than in most other unfriendly treatments of him.[34] His physical aspect is quite unattractive: he is emaciated, and his face seems jaundiced; his sinister eyes resemble those of a hyena; he has deep wrinkles, and his forehead and cheeks show the imprint of "ardent passions"; finally, his red, sparse hair and puny beard give him a "strange and ambiguous expression" (p. 387).

We enter his thoughts, seeing his ambition, his desire to add Portugal to his possessions, and his fear of death. On this evening, as he watches the sunset from the balcony of his palace, he is reminded of death and breaks out in a cold sweat. But Philip is also in love. The object of his passion is the beautiful Princess of Eboli, whose palace is quite close to his own. This same evening he looks at her balconies and sees the form of a man who is visting the Princess. The King suspects that it

is the hated Juan de Escobedo, secretary of his half-brother
Don John of Austria. Philip thinks that Don John, who rules
Flanders in the name of the King, has dangerous ambitions of
his own and writes secret instructions to Escobedo, which the
latter always keeps on his person in a green portfolio. Thus
the King is driven to murder through two motives, the desire
to know what the correspondence between Don John and Escobedo contains and the desire to eliminate a rival for the favors
of his beloved Princess. In a dramatic scene, which is moreover
in dialogue form, Philip gives instructions to his secretary Antonio Pérez, another unsavory personage who is also infatuated
with the Princess. The instructions, although not spelled out
for us, since according to the narrator the King speaks in a low
voice, clearly point to the murder of Escobedo. Something of
the epic fierceness of Don Pedro the Cruel lights up in Philip
when Pérez asks his royal master for a written order. Like a
"ferocious tiger" who looks at a "rat," Philip gives him the order
and then grips his arm with a hand which is "stronger than
tongs." He looks at him with "eyes from hell," saying: "Secret
and speed, / And it is I who charge you with it" (p. 390).[35]

   The next subdivision, entitled "La cartera verde" ("The Green
Portfolio") takes place in the Palace of Eboli, where the King
is paying a visit to the Princess. The latter is terrified of Philip
and hopes he will leave soon. But the King asks her to play the
lute, and she complies. With great skill, as always, Rivas weaves
together elements giving a sinister air to the scene: The "infernal
smile" on the lips of Philip; the wind coming across the balcony
and shaking the candles, causing the furniture and hangings to
take on fantastic shapes; the silent prayer of both King and
Princess as the church bells call for the evening prayers; the cry
in the distance; the arrival of Pérez with the green portfolio, on
which can be seen a drop of blood, and the fainting spell of the
Princess. Finally, we learn that the body of Juan de Escobedo
was found the next morning. The *romance* has been all the
more effective because we do not witness any violence. The
murder has taken place off stage, and we only see the results.
The poem ends on a slightly ironic note as the author asks himself where the three men met after death and concludes that
it must have been in hell.

It is perhaps surprising that a nationalist, and by now a conservative, like Rivas chose to portray Philip II in an essentially
negative light, though a certain Satanic grandeur at times emanates from this figure. After all, under Philip II, Spain was
immensely powerful and universally feared. The answer lies
perhaps in the impact made on the poet by the bad reputation
which Philip II enjoyed with the European Enlightenment and
with Spanish liberals—a reputation still widely accepted by the
Spain of the 1830's which had only recently suffered under
another despot, Ferdinand VII. The rehabilitation of Philip
II, begun in the later nineteenth century,[36] reached a climax
during the Franco years when Philip was consistently portrayed
as the good, "prudent" king.

One of the most interesting of all the *romances*, in spite of the
fact that it is probably completely fictitious, is "El cuento de un
veterano" ("A Veteran's Tale"), written in Gibraltar in 1837.
It is a good story which combines the element of the macabre
with that of suspense, and despite its obvious implausibility it
holds our attention. One of the figures in the tale is a young
Spanish officer, Don Juan Enríquez de Lara, who serves in the
Spanish armies fighting the Austrians in Italy in the 1740's.
This young man is a Don Juan figure, described as a "horse
without bridle, / A devil in human form / When it is a question of love, / When a lady attracts him" (p. 403). This officer,
like the traditional Don Juan, reaps his punishment, though in
quite different form from that in Tirso de Molina's seventeenth-
century masterpiece.

Lara is billeted in Parma in a house which faces a convent.
As he looks out at that building from his balcony, he hears
the voice of a nun who calls out to him from behind her
Venetian blind and throws in his direction a paper in which
she indicates her desire to meet him. If he wants to see her,
all he has to do is to attend a party given that same afternoon
by the convent in honor of his regiment's colonel. She will hold
a rose in her hand to identify herself. Lara now remembers
that a girl whom he had deceived in Rome had spoken to him
about a sister who, abandoned by her lover, had been forced
to enter a convent in Parma. A great adventure seems to await
him. Naturally he goes to the convent and sees among the

nuns a most beautiful young woman with a rose in her hand. Lara cannot take his eyes off her, and the narrator remarks ominously: "He was like the bird / Under the tyrannical attraction / Of the eyes of the serpent, / Whose food it will be" (p. 405).

The nun, taking advantage of the party, is able to hand the handsome officer a note in which she asks him for protection, since she is in the convent against her will, and begs him to visit her that same night. Lara, back in his lodging, hesitates. He realizes that he would commit a sacrilege if he climbed the wall of the convent. The religious element comes into play now, and we are reminded somewhat of the warnings given several times to the Don Juan of Tirso de Molina's *El burlador de Sevilla* (*The Trickster of Seville*) when the narrator says: "For there is no moment / When human existence is assured, / And eternal Justice / Knows and punishes everything" (p. 407). We are even more strikingly reminded of Tirso de Molina's Don Juan by the quatrain "And at his young age, with his health and vigor / He considers that the moment / At which it is sufficient for man to repent / In order to save himself / Is far away" (p. 407). The quatrain's theme repeats the whole idea of Tirso de Molina's Don Juan's "Qué largo me lo fiáis" (literally, "How long you extend my debt," or "I have a long time to repent").

After climbing the walls of the convent Lara is taken by the nun to her cell. Once there she serves him pastry and wine while she takes only water, claiming that she is not used to alcohol. She then bids him open a closet, out of which falls the corpse of a richly dressed man. With a voice which seems like the roar of a tigress or the "cry of a hungry hyena" she explains to the young man that the dead man had been her lover but had married another woman. She had been forced to take refuge in the convet but had been able to lure her former lover to her cell where she had killed him. And now, backing up her words with a pistol, she demands that Lara help her bury him.

Powerless, Don Juan obeys her and buries the corpse in the garden. For some time now the young officer has felt unwell. The nun notices his condition and now tells him that she has also avenged her sister, whom Don Juan had deceived in Rome as he had many other women. As he makes his way back over the wall in a state of torpor, the nun, who fittingly has expressed herself with a "satanic laughter," and who seems to have turned into a "fury," informs her guest that his wine had been poisoned. Back in the street Don Juan collapses and dies.

This tale, even more than the other *romances*, is obviously full of Romantic ingredients, notwithstanding its echoes of the Baroque drama *El burlador de Sevilla*. We have a young girl, abandoned by her lover, who has to enter a convent. A young man visits a convent at night. There is the element of vengeance, which is carried out by means of poison. There is death and burial at night. There is the contrast between the religious state and the beauty of the young nun on the one hand, and her thirst for vengeance on the other, which gives her a demonic quality. Finally the story is highly implausible, but this does not prevent us from following its development with interest.

IV *Painter-Poet*

Rivas' talent as a painter was not confined to his brush. He shines as a painter in much of his poetic production. But perhaps nowhere does this gift appear with a stronger impact than in the *Romances históricos*. Striking descriptions abound in this collection. The ability of the poet to present beautiful tableaux is illustrated again and again. Let us consider for instance the description of King Pedro the Cruel and the Mayor of Seville in "Una antigualla de Sevilla." The picture conveys perfectly the awe and respect in which Don Pedro was held by his subjects: On the one side, seated in an armchair, is the King, soberly described as a "young man with a graceful figure," and on the other, "At a reverent distance, / One knee on the ground, / Dressed in a black robe, / With a white beard and white hair, / And with the staff of mayor / Rendering homage to the supreme power, / Martín Fernández Cerón / Was an emblem of respect" (p. 314). We note the use of black and white, two colors which are employed with great frequency in these poems.

In the same *romance* another tableau makes an important contribution to the creation of the sinister atmosphere of the torture chamber to which the old woman is dragged. It is a picture devoid of colors except for black and white and the hint of red through the mention of blood:

> In an armchair, on a stand of tiers,
> There can be seen dressed in black
> The good mayor Cerón,
> With grave brow and stern face.
>
> At his side, on a desk
> Which looks more like a tomb,
> An old notary prepares
> His parchments and his pens.
>
> And in the middle of that room
> There can be seen a bed of planks
> Dirty with blood, and its curtains
> Are ropes, hooks, pulleys.
>
> Next to it two executioners
> With an imbecile and robust appearance
> Prepare from a bag of leather
> Iron tools of sinister appearance. (p. 315)

The power and wealth of Don Alvaro de Luna are well expressed in the following description of his attire in the *romance* "Don Alvaro de Luna." Let us note that a few more colors than in the preceding tableau are present here:

> A coat of green fabric
> Adorned with golden braid
> Is his dress, and he wears on his shoulders,
> Whiter than hermin
>
> A large cloak in whose folds
> A red cross indicative
> Of his rank of grand master of Santiago[37]
> Is seen splendidly embroidered,
>
> And a bonnet of black velvet
> With embroidered cocks,
> But without plumage
> Is the shelter of his head. (p. 330)

Toward the end of the same *romance* there is a splendid description of the scaffold on which Don Alvaro de Luna will be beheaded. The objects described fit in perfectly with the grim developments which are the subject of this ballad:

> On it is placed
> An altar on the right,
> Covered with velvet;
> And surrounded by yellow candles,
>
> Whose light the sun dims
> And the wind prevents from burning,
> A silver crucifix
> Appears on a cross of ebony.
>
> To the left
> There lies a humble coffin;
> Near it is seen a tenterhook
> On a pillar of wood,
>
> And in the middle, firmly, a chopping block,
> And in front a black pillow,
> And an ax, on whose blade
> The sun's rays are reflected. (p. 333).

At times the poet vividly expresses his joy at being able to present us with a description. The satisfaction of creating a tableau is eloquently voiced in the following passage from "La buenaventura" ("The Fortune"):

> Magnificent was the scenery,
> Superb the panorama,
> A grandiose spectacle
> Which dazzled his eyes:
>
> The river covered with ships
> Of a thousand friendly nations
> With streamers, pennants,
> Bannerols and emblems,
>
> Where splendid colors
> Shine with the setting sun,
> Where gentle winds stir,
> Where breezes frolic. (p. 354)

The description continues with an account of all the things and all the people that could be seen on the ships and on both banks of the Guadalquivir River. To convey to us the intense activity as well as the denseness of the crowds, the narrator makes use of accumulation. The longest accumulation of substantives, sometimes accompanied by adjectives, in the whole collection of *romances* gives us the feeling of swarming life. There are eight quatrains involved, which would have formed one continuous whole without one single finite verb form had it not been for two quatrains in the middle, one of which does show one finite verb form and the other a present participle. The following is an example: "Moors, *moriscos*[38] and Greeks, / Egyptians, Israelites, / Black men, whites, old, young, / Speaking different languages" (p. 354).

One of the most painterly passages and one of the best of the collection is found in the *romance* "Un castellano leal." In the second subdivision of this poem we have a tableau of Charles V (1517–56) which is actually the description of the portrait of Charles by Titian in the Prado Museum of Madrid. The emperor is seen standing in front of an armchair and at the side of a table. He wears a German tabard of gold and silver brocade, garnished with sable, as well as a waistcoat of bright yellow satin, covered with exquisite embroidery. On his chest hangs the insignia of the Golden Fleece.[39] He wears "A velvet cap / With a wide egret, fixed / By a diamond jewel / And an antique cameo / ... On his hip / He has placed his powerful right hand, / Which clasps two amber gloves / And an exquisite flytrap" (p. 373). True, the poet had the actual portrait in front of him, yet the detailed description with its several colors—gold, silver yellow, white, amber—gives us a vivid tableau of the powerful, elegantly attired emperor.

In "El Conde de Villamediana," published in 1833, which relates the death in 1622 of Don Juan de Tarsis, Count of Villamediana, purportedly the lover of the queen, at the hand of an assassin hired by King Philip IV (1621–65), there is a passage which brings to life some of the most prestigious figures of the Spanish Baroque period. During a fiesta in the palace of the Retiro in Madrid we get a glimpse of several poets, among them the great Lope de Vega. His hair and his moustache are

"White as pure snow; / And through his clerical dress / One recognizes that as a young man he had been a warrior. / His chest is adorned with the insignia / Of the Order of the Hospitalers, / And in his eyes there burns a fire / Which makes gods out of men" (p. 398).

One of the most effective tableaux, which conveys all the horror of the situation of the young rake, is found in "El cuento de un veterano." In the last *romance* of the group comprising the poem the nun is seen, covered with her veil and her cloak, like a "frightful ghost." "In her hand she holds a lantern, / Which leaves her body hidden in vague shadows, / And with the light of hell illuminates / At her feet, in front of her, / A ditch or tomb, / Which Don Juan is making deeper with a spade" (p. 411). The poet-painter is aware of the pictorial quality of this scene and adds: "On one of its edges can be seen / The corpse, and it is / A strange, frightening *picture*,[40] / With an effect which sets the hair on end."

In the *Historical Ballads* we find the brilliant color effects of some of the poet's earlier work: the same clouds of gold and red of the sunset, the same golds, reds and purples of the dress of kings and nobles, the faces of rose and jasmine, the noble blue eyes which we have met before. But as Allison Peers has noted, "bursts of brilliance are not the characteristic of the color-scheme of the *romances*. Rather are the poems marked by the continual invasion of white and black. Whole pages follow in succession in which no other color is seen."[41] Perhaps many of the scenes Rivas described are less apt to be rendered in colors than those of *El moro expósito*. Perhaps, too, the rapid octosyllable was a factor in preventing Rivas from fully expressing his taste for colors.

Although there are many descriptive passages, perhaps as a result of Rivas' penchant for detail in description, metaphors and comparisons are relatively few in number. It is as if the poet, by concentrating all his talent on describing reality, had foregone the use of imagery. There are a few more comparisons than metaphors. Rather than employing the metaphor for poetic effect, Rivas generally prefers to separate neatly image from reality, a process more attractive to the logical mind of the

Neoclassicist than the use of the metaphor. This preference for
the simple comparison, which can also be noted in *The Foundling
Moor*, is possibly a carryover from his Neoclassic days. The comparison, often implicit, is used to provide a striking illumination of
the reality described. When speaking for instance of Pedro the
Cruel in "El alcázar de Sevilla," as he paces the floor, the poet
says: "Thus have I seen the ferocious tiger, / Now calm, now
enraged, / Move to and fro on all sides / Within the narrow cage"
(p. 320). A little further on we have a striking comparison when
the thoughts that swirl around Don Pedro are compared to birds
of prey: "Just as around the lonely tower / Are flying / Fierce
birds of prey, / When the sun is about to set, / Thus around
Don Pedro / There fly various thoughts" (p. 320).

In the following instance, found in "El solemne desengaño,"
where the poet tries to show us that there can be no healthy
body with a sick soul, the images evoked by the process of
comparison have a function which transcends that of creating
a poetic illumination of the concept on the plane of reality.
There is more involved than the mere evocation of an image
for poetic effect. This is because on the real plane the poet
makes an effort to explain, to teach a lesson. Thus the creation
of the imagery is really subordinated to the didactic intent.
This didactic element is another example of the lingering influence of Neoclassic art on Rivas' craft:

> The most luxuriant lily,
> Choicest part of the garden,
> Bows its neck if it hides
> A gnawing worm in its bosom.
>
> And the strongest oak
> Which points its splendor at the sky,
> Breaks under the gust of the wind
> If its heart dries up.
>
> Thus with a sick soul
> There cannot be a healthy body,
> Nor health which does not collapse
> As a result of a broken heart. (p. 376)

It has been said that Rivas, himself a painter, sees life not as something dynamic but rather as something static. "All his works are visions of one unique moment," says Azorín, "or series of independent moments. There is no movement in the aesthetic conception of Saavedra; when the poet wants to give us movement, the concatenation of things, the evolution of an event or of a life, then he fails."[42] We do not agree with this view. With specific reference to the *Historical Ballads* it is true that Rivas gives us normally a series of scenes; but one does not have the feeling of jumping from one isolated moment to another self-contained situation when reading these poems. There is no feeling of over-fragmentation. The narration on the whole proceeds smoothly. Only rarely do we have the feeling that one particular moment has not been sufficiently prepared by what precedes. We might compare the art of Rivas in the *romances* not to the projection of slides, which indeed would be a static precedure, but to cinematography. We realize that in the art of the film there are also techniques which tend to undermine dynamic flow through over-fragmentation. But this is not the case in most of the episodes in the *Romances históricos*. Time and again a series of episodes arrayed in a logical sequence gives us a smooth-flowing narrative whole.

In "Una antigualla de Sevilla" we see essentially four moments of a film: The duel in the street, Don Pedro and the Mayor, Don Pedro's activities after the conversation with the Mayor, and the dénouement in the jail. It is a story in which the different elements just mentioned are logically linked, mesh perfectly, and form an ongoing narrative. Similarly, in "El fratricidio," we have first the conversation between Claquín and Sanabria, then a vision of the castle, next the nightmare of the King, and finally the death of Don Pedro. There is no feeling of a lack of dynamic progression, of linkage. The same thing can be said of other *romances*: In "Un castellano leal," we have first the order of the Count of Benavente to close his palace to the Duke of Borbón, then the description of Charles V and the Count of Benavente, followed by the conversation between Benavente and the Emperor, and finally the burning of Benavente's palace. The four scenes follow each other logically and smoothly. It is a perfect little film. Rivas' talent for what

we would call today cinematographic art can be seen in most
of the *romances*.[43]

Something which Azorín did not fully develop in the previously quoted passage, but which can be deduced from his
words, is that Rivas painted tableaux rather than dynamic scenes.
True, Rivas provides many beautiful tableaux. We have only
to think of the description of the castle of Montiel in "El
fratricidio," the description of Charles V in "Un castellano leal,"
that of the Guadalquivir in "La buenaventura," etc. But at the
same time it cannot be denied that many passages are full of
movement, contributing to the dynamic flow of many episodes.
"El alcázar de Sevilla," for instance, has a few tableaux; but
the murder of Don Fadrique and that of his servant, as well
as the comings and goings of Don Pedro at the end, impart
sufficient movement to the poem and form a striking contrast
with the more static scenes. In "Don Alvaro de Luna," the
arrival of the royal favorite in Valladolid is full of movement,
as is the scene of the execution, although the latter, because
of the quiet courage shown by Luna, could perhaps be compared to a slow-motion sequence. There is action in the nocturnal
duel in "La buenaventura," though this *romance* also has a
number of rather static moments. The battles between Spaniards
and Frenchmen are narrated in dynamic fashion in "Amor,
honor y valor" and "La victoria de Pavía," although more in the
latter than in the former. There is movement in the bullfight
in "El Conde de Villamediana," and "El cuento de un veterano,"
with its vengeful nun, is a combination of tableaux and dynamic scenes.

In "Bailén" we have the whole passage, full of movement,
which deals with the rapid arming of Seville. We see Napoleon's
armies flood Spain like a torrent. There is also action in the
shock of the two armies, when the French, unable to break
through the Spanish lines, "Falter / And struggle in vain; / They
withdraw, men and horses fall to the ground" (p. 417). Then
Rivas beautifully combines pictorial and dynamic ingredients
in the next four lines which refer to the French standards with
their eagles as emblems: "Y las águilas altivas / Humillan el
vuelo raudo, / Ensangrentadas sus plumas / Hasta perderse en
el fango" ("And the haughty eagles, / Their plumes stained

with blood, / Falter in their impetuous flight / Until they flounder in the mud," p. 417).

Throughout the *romances* the author makes extensive use of the devices of anaphora and accumulation, examples of which we have already seen. Sometimes these devices, designed to extract maximum poetic effect, tend to lend movement to a scene. A case in point is "Recuerdos de un grande hombre" ("Recollections of a Great Man"). While describing Cordova, which Ferdinand and Isabella have made their headquarters for the coming campaign against Granada, Rivas writes the following quatrains, in which we note anaphora, accumulation, and the absence of verbs except for *ser* in the first line. The net result is that the author effectively conveys a sense of dynamic activity to the reader:

Todo es movimiento y vida,	Everything is movement and life,
todo actividad extraña,	Everything is a strange activity,
todo bélico aparato,	Everything a martial preparation,
todo fiestas cortesanas.	Everything courtly fiestas.
Todo es riqueza y aliento,	Everything is wealth and activity,
todo brocados y holandas,	Everything brocade and fine Dutch linen,
todo confusión alegre,	Everything a happy confusion,
todo caprichos y galas	Everything fancy and ostentation.

(p. 339)

It should also be noted that offsetting the lack of movement in a number of scenes is the presence throughout the *romances* of another dimension, that of dramatic tension. Scenes full of dramatic tension abound to the extent that one critic has stated, exaggerating somewhat, that "actually the *Historical Ballads* are simply a wonderful collection of dramas . . . , written in dialogue in many parts."[44] Let us recall the dialogue between Don Pedro and the Mayor in "Una antigualla de Sevilla" ("An Old Tale of Seville"); the confrontation of the two brothers in "El fratricidio," ending in the death of Don Pedro; the conversation between Isabella and Columbus in "Recuerdos de un grande hombre"; the confrontation between the French king and the Spanish ambassador in "Un embajador español";

and the dialogue between Philip II and Antonio Pérez in "Una noche de Madrid en 1578." This latter *romance* has another scene that is intensely dramatic: the whole episode of the visit of the King to the Princess of Eboli. It is a magnificent moment in which the emotions of the actors involved vibrate under a thin veneer of outward calm. There is not much action, and yet we feel the violence of the murder, which reaches us only through a cry in the night.

V *Conclusion*

This then is an overview of the *Romances históricos*. As we noted earlier these poems must be considered Rivas' greatest contribution to Spanish Romanticism. Here his narrative and pictorial genius is at his best. With an extraordinary eye for the striking scene as well as for the picturesque detail the poet transports us to some key episodes of Spanish history and makes us relive heroic and macabre moments from the fourteenth century down to the nineteenth century. Whether he is depicting a bullfight in the time of Philip IV, the slaying of Pedro the Cruel by his half-brother, or the decisive battle of Bailén, Rivas, always in full command of his material and using the Spanish octosyllable in virtuoso fashion, succeeds, as few historians have succeeded, in brilliantly re-creating the heroic as well as the macabre past and in giving the reader a colorful pageant of Spanish history.

CHAPTER 6

Religion and Nationalism: The Leyendas

I *General Observations*

R IVAS' last important poetic productions appeared in 1854. In this year he published as part of his collected edition three narrative poems which he entitled *Leyendas* (*Legends*). Two of them, *La azucena milagrosa* (*The Miraculous Lily*) and *Maldonado*, each quite long, had been written in Naples in 1847[1] and in Madrid in 1852 respectively. The shorter poem *El aniversario* (*The Anniversary*) was composed in Madrid in May, 1854.

It is not easy to distinguish this genre from Riva's earlier *Romances históricos* (*Historical Ballads*), especially from those that are of a completely fictitious nature. The nineteenth-century Spanish author and critic Eugenio de Ochoa calls the *leyenda* a novel in verse.[2] Manuel Cañete calls it a "type of traditional tale generally written in a variety of meters and usually designed to awaken pleasant memories or to offer agreeable entertainment."[3] It is true that the *leyendas* are written in a great variety of meters, while the ballads are composed with few exceptions in the *verso de romance* (*octosyllabic assonance*). We might also say that the *leyendas* are looser in structure and generally less epic. But in two of the *leyendas* (*La azucena milagrosa* and *Maldonado*) we find epic passages which could very well fit into the structure of a *romance*, as well as moments of high dramatic intensity comparable to those found in many a ballad. We find in *La azucena milagrosa* and *Maldonado* a fervent nationalism, but we have also determined this to be an important aspect of the *romances*. *El aniversario* has a rather macabre ending which reminds us of this important characteristic of so many *romances*.

115

It will be recalled that Rivas gave the subtitle of *leyenda* to his *El moro expósito* (*The Foundling Moor*). It would be tempting then to consider these three *leyendas* similar in nature to Rivas' longest poetic work. True, the *Moro* is written in one meter, the *romance heroico*,[4] while the *leyendas* are composed in a variety of meters, although there are quite a few passages in the *leyendas* which are also written in that meter. On the other hand, like the *Moro*, two of the *leyendas* at least, *Maldonado* and *El aniversario* (*The Anniversary*), appear to be based on some sort of popular tradition.

And yet, aside from the question of the meters involved, there is an important difference between the *leyendas* and both the *Moro* and the *romances*. In the *leyendas* the supernatural plays an important role, while in the *Moro* and the *romances* its role is negligible.[5] The reason for this lies in the fact that as Rivas advanced in years his religiosity, at the same time as his conservative inclinations in politics, became more ardent; nowhere do we see his religious faith expressed as intensely as in the *leyendas*, especially in *La azucena milagrosa*. This is to our view the main factor separating these works from the earlier ones. Rivas is still Romantic in the *leyendas*, but his Romanticism, more than ever before, has become tinged with religious fanaticism. What was Romantic patriotism in the *romances* has now become fused with an intense faith which fairly exudes religious intolerance. We are far removed from the Rivas of *Don Alvaro* and its links, however tenuous, with "Byronic" Romanticism. If in *Don Alvaro* the author echoed to a certain extent the Romanticism of some of the great European Romantics, in the *leyendas* he is a nationalist utterly dedicated to Catholicism. Let us now analyze the three *leyendas*.

II   *La azucena milagrosa*

A. The Plot

While the young nobleman Nuño Garcerán is away fighting the Moors of Granada, Rodrigo, his administrator and friend, tries to seduce Nuño's wife Blanca. The faithful wife rebuffs him. Rodrigo decides to avenge himself and upon Nuño's return from the war convinces him that she is having an affair. Seeing her in the company of her young brother, whom he had never met before, Nuño thinks that this is the lover; he kills her and seriously wounds the young man, whereupon a violent storm destroys his castle and ravages his fields. After spending the next thirty-three years in Mexico and taking part in its conquest, Nuño returns to Spain and in a field near Seville comes upon a skull which turns out to be that of the villainous Rodrigo. The skull explains that God has given him permission to tell Nuño the truth, which he proceeds to do. Nuño, shattered by the skull's revelations, next meets a monk who, as chance has it, is the brother of Blanca. The monk tells him that he must return to his land and go through years of penance, after which he will be pardoned by God and admitted to Heaven. Nuño does penance for five years in a cave. He is then taken by a white deer to a chapel containing an image of the Virgin, who tells him that he has been forgiven. The fields of Nuño's estate now become fertile again and on the tomb of his wife there grows a lily. As Nuño plucks the flower he dies and his soul flies to Heaven. Finally, Blanca's brother is ordered by Heaven to erect a monastery to the Virgin on the spot where Nuño had died. Helped by the faithful he carries out this project. In the monastery, at the foot of the Virgin's image, the miraculous lily, which has returned from Heaven, now spreads its perfume through the air. The narrator informs us that the monastery was destroyed during the War of Independence against Napoleon, but that the lily was seen flying to Heaven.

B. Analysis

The theme of the husband convinced by a villain that his wife had been unfaithful to him, only to discover his mistake after taking vengeance, is not original. Moreover, Rivas considerably dilutes this theme by the addition of extraneous elements. For instance, the motif of the lily, on which the story ends, has no essential connection with the main theme. The story is pervaded by an intense religious feeling. Expressions of ardent faith abound, mingled on occasion with fanatical intolerance and with patriotism. When referring to the recently conquered Granada, the narrator says:

The amazed world,
Seeing her with profound respect,
With the Catholic faith in her bosom,
Once stained with the filthy slime
Of infamous ceremonies and rites
Condemned by Heaven,
And hearing in her mosques
To the terror of horrible hell
The holy words
Of the holy Gospel,
Which encourages the slave and tames the tyrant,
Instead of the blasphemies of Mahomet.[6]

The one epic passage of the poem, fittingly written in the
romance heroico, deals with the discovery of the New World
and the conquest of Mexico. It is profoundly patriotic, and its
hero is Cortés:

The one who carried the cross of his banner
From triumph to triumph, conquering, august,
From the fertile plain of Tabasco
To the high towers of Cholula,

With only six hundred Spaniards
Tamed the fury of a hundred thousand warriors,
By dint of constancy and bravery
In the deep valleys of Otumba,

And intrepidly planted the Hispanic flag,
To the eternal glory of his Fatherland,
In opulent Mexico, which the world
Calls the empress of the West. (p. 438)

Much of the religious fervor of the poet is directed toward
the Virgin. She is mentioned a number of times in *La azucena
milagrosa* and always with the utmost devotion. She is the
"mother of the Word" (426), the "Sovereign Virgin, who is
the queen of angels," the "Virgin, refuge and protectress of that
land," the "Virgin without stain" (p. 451), and the "pure Virgin"
(p. 452).

The present occasionally displaces the past, momentarily at

least, in the *romances* and *leyendas*, as if the poet wanted to
underscore the continuous flow of History. In *The Miraculous
Lily*, in the midst of this religious and patriotic fervor, we find
a curious anti-American and anti-British note. On speaking of
Mexico the poet suddenly remembers that that land, once conquered for Castile by the hero Cortés is now the "unhappy
prey / Of an infidel, upstart, obscure race, / Which insults with
its heretical dogmas / The faith of the glorious Recaredo" (p.
438).[7] The allusion is of course to the Mexican-American War of
1846–48, which was going badly for Mexico by the time this
leyenda was written. And is there not one single drop of Castilian
blood left that will smite the aggression of this "race of mer-
chants," the poet asks himself? Yes, there is, but it is shed
without force or power. Rebellions, dissensions, ambitions,
fostered by perfidious Albion, are weakening those "unhappy
people, / Who are children and think they are men" (p. 438).
Obviously Rivas realized that Spain was incapable of influencing
the march of events in Mexico, for after asking himself why Spain
is not flying to the rescue of her child, "forgiving the offenses like
a mother," he is forced to conclude: "Enough, and let an im-
penetrable veil / Cover the miseries / Which rob my Fatherland
of its power, / And cloud the glory of its name" (p. 438).

The intense religious feeling of the author is not limited to
expressions of devotion but is also expressed through the dual
structure of the poem. *The Miraculous Lily* is written on two
planes, the real and the supernatural. The reality of the villainy
of Rodrigo, of the jealousy of Garcerán, of the crime of Garcerán, and of his repentance, is balanced by the supernatural
elements, which include the sudden and devastating hurricane
after the death of Blanca, the encounter with the skull, the
episode of the deer, the appearance of the lily (symbol of
Garcerán's redemption), and its continuous presence at the foot
of the image of the Virgin. Actually we might divide the poem
into two parts according to the appearance of the supernatural
ingredient. Except for the incident of the sudden storm which
destroys Garcerán's castle and devastates his fields, the events
up to the hero's return from Mexico are related on the plane of
reality. After his return, however, the real and the supernatural
are continuously juxtaposed until the very end of the story. At

times the two planes seem to merge. For instance, after Garcerán
is granted forgiveness by the Virgin, he has a series of visions.
With regard to the first one, at least, we cannot be absolutely
sure whether it is a purely subjective vision or whether there is
an intrusion by an objective experience. We are told that the
hermit,

> Clinging to a cross,
> Went up to Heaven,
> And happily lost himself
> In seas of happiness
> And in fields of eternal light,
>
> Breathing in the aromas
> of heavenly gardens,
> And enjoying that perfume
> Of the pure and soft breath
> Of the holy seraphim. (p. 452)

The over-all impression the reader derives from this continuous juxtaposition of the real and the supernatural is that
of an ardent yet touching faith. It might be easy for the reader
to dismiss all the religious embroidery as superstition or even
religious fanaticism, but it is difficult not to be touched at
times by the candid faith which is expressed so lyrically by our
author. It often seems as if we were transported to the Baroque,
when the metaphysical intruded so much upon the physical. But
essentially Rivas narrates the events of this *leyenda* with the
simple faith of a medieval storyteller rather than with the more
sophisticated feelings of a Baroque writer.

Yet while it is tempting to point out the medieval tone of
this poem, it is important to keep in mind its Romantic aspects.
As we have seen, the supernatural itself was highly favored by
Romantic poets. Thus it can be viewed both as a traditional
Spanish element and a Romantic ingredient. But there are other
Romantic traits in *The Miraculous Lily*: The description of
Blanca, as Nuño sees her upon his return from the wars, is
highly Romantic. She appears as a delicate, virginal form, pale
and with a noble and celestial expression. She reminds us of
the many Romantic heroines who seem to float between two
worlds:[8]

A svelte, elegant figure,
And delicate forms,
Which shine, adorned
With garments of virginal whiteness;

And a pale face
On a flexible neck,
So beautiful and tranquil,
And with such a noble and celestial expression. (p. 435)

The hurricane which destroys Garcerán's castle is described as a cataclysmic event in the spirit of Romantic exaggeration. The adjectives "frightful," referring to the clouds, "impalpable," speaking of the darkness, "tremendous," alluding to the horrible spectacle, and "fearful," referring to the thunderclap, underline the awesome power of the unleashed elements. The Romantics are fond of having nature give resonance to the actions of the hero. Here, though the storm is supernatural in nature, it fits into this Romantic mold, for it echoes the crime of the protagonist. It also brings from the poet an allusion to the Bible. Garcerán, who has just committed a foul deed and who flees from God's wrath, is appropriately compared to Cain, "the first killer," upon whom the world looked as he was "enveloped in frightful storms" (p. 437).

Ghosts, dear to Romanticism, are also present in *La azucena milagrosa (The Miraculous Lily)*. After the terrible storm there can be seen "whitish phantasms moving through the silent darkness," and moans as well as "pitiful voices" can be heard (p. 445). And when Garcerán lives in the cave as a hermit doing penance for his crime he spends his nights "surrounded by specters and phantasms, / By visions and goblins" (p. 447). One of the most Romantic passages is found in this same episode, with Garcerán in the cave pursued by all sorts of visions and temptations which impede his progress toward purification. The author comes perilously close to a caricature of the melancholy Romantic spending his time in inhospitable surroundings:

How many times upon the lugubrious
Death of a beautiful day,
When the dying sun

> Wrapped its locks
> In fervid vapors
> Like a pallid corpse
>
> .   .   .   .
>
> Did the gloomy penitent,
> On a high cliff,
> His face bathed in melancholy,
> His forehead bent,
> Wander through an immense
> Number of memories. (p. 447)

The visions and the temptations which assail Garcerán during his probationary period contrast sharply with those that he experiences after he has been forgiven. This contrast, a device dear to Romanticism and to Rivas, is seen for instance in the two different visions of Blanca. During his penance Garcerán sees his former wife looking through broken clouds full of lightning, scooping blood from the wound in her chest and hurling it onto his forehead while shouting: "No, you cursed one, / For your crime /There is no forgiveness. / God, in his anger, / Has uttered his damnation. / Go down with Rodrigo, / For neither one do I forgive, both I curse" (p. 449).

The later appearance of Blanca is quite different. This beatific vision is quite in keeping with the change that has occurred in Garcerán's status: "And on her chest, where the wound / Had been inflicted by the homicidal dagger, / She showed a bright ruby / Like a red star, / with reflections of eternal life." And Garcerán thinks she told him on leaving him: "Come, Garcerán. Why does your love / Take so long in coming to me? / Come up to a better life. / What keeps you back and makes you afraid? / Come, for the Lord is waiting for you" (p. 453). It is passages like this last one which convey to us all the naive but touching faith of the poet.

We have noted that Rivas occasionally comments upon the present in the midst of his dealings with the past. Aside from the comment on the Mexican-American War, there is a lyrical outburst in which the poet expresses all his love for his beloved Seville. Far from Spain, residing in Naples, Rivas recalls the queen city of Andalusia with words bathed in Romantic nostalgia:

> Seville! Oh magic name, which enchants
> My mind with its peaceful sound,
> And which surrounds with placid recollections
> My icy heart and my memory!
>
> Seville, queen with the pleasant climate
> In which the Guadalquivir shows off
> Its royal splendor, flowing towards the sea
> Where the sun hides and turns its back on Europe.
>
> (p. 437)

One more word about *The Miraculous Lily*, relative to its metrical variety, which is more noticeable than in the other two *leyendas*. At the beginning, the introduction which describes the happy life of Garcerán and Blanca and his departure for the war is written in the epic *octava real* meter (stanzas of eight hendecasyllables rhyming *abababcc*). Garcerán's sojourn in Granada is told in *silvas*, combinations of hendecasyllables and heptasyllables. Later we have among other forms the *romance heroico*, which we have already met in *El moro expósito (The Foundling Moor)*, the *romance* meter in the story told by the skull and in the episode of the deer, and *quintillas* or stanzas of five *octosyllables*, rhyming either *abaab* or *abbab*.[9]

III Maldonado

A. The Plot

This story too has a medieval setting. The Aragonese admiral Pérez de Aldana, insulted by the Duke of Normandy in a church near Barcelona, challenges the Frenchman to a duel in Paris. The combat takes place before a huge throng and in the presence of the King of France, father of the Duke. Aldana is the victor and is about to kill his fallen enemy when the King of France asks him to spare his son in return for anything the Aragonese might ask. All Aldana asks is to take home with him the five golden lilies, emblems of the French monarchy, which he had knocked off the Duke's shield during the combat. The courtiers around the King and the Duke himself raise an outcry, but the King, having made a promise, feels compelled by his sense of honor to yield to the Spaniard's demand. As he agrees to hand over the five lilies his son exclaims: "C'est mal donné" (literally, It is badly given), to which Aldana replies that from now on, to commemorate this grudge and his victory, his family name will be Maldonado, which is the Spanish equivalent of the French "mal donné."

B. Analysis

In a note to the first edition the author indicated that the subject of this *leyenda* was suggested to him by a good friend who had found it in an old Aragonese archive. Thus the story seems based on some kind of local tradition. The differences between it and the *Romances historicos* (*Historical Ballads*) may not seem clear at first sight. Yet there are aspects which set it apart from this genre: First the metrical variety, not as extensive as in *La azucena milagrosa* (*The Miraculous Lily*), is still striking. We go from the *romance heroico* at the beginning to the simple *romance* meter, to the *redondilla* (*octosílabos* rhyming *abba*),[10] to the *octava real*, this latter meter being used for the description of the combat between Aldana and the Duke of Normandy, while the octosyllabic *redondilla* is used for the dialogues in the dramatic scenes.

Secondly, and more importantly, this *leyenda* contains some religious and supernatural elements. They are much less decisive than in *The Miraculous Lily*, but are nevertheless noticeable. The Aragonese fleet, returning to Barcelona from its victories over the Moors, runs into a terrible storm. Admiral Pérez de Aldana, wounded in the battle against the infidels, falls to his knees imploring the Virgin to save the fleet. "Holy Virgin" and "Pure Virgin," he exclaims, showing us once more that, as in *La azucena*, the Mother of God is the object of the poet's reverence. If his prayers are heard he will go to the temple of the Sierra of Monserrate and place the captured flags in front of the Virgin's altar. The prayers are heard. Miraculously the storm ends and the fleet is saved.

The episode of the pilgrimage to the temple of the Virgin in the Sierra de Monserrate, however, could easily form part of a *romance histórico*. It is written in the *romance* meter and gives Rivas the opportunity to show once more his talent for description. Anaphora and accumulation contribute as usual to the vividness of the picture, to the sensation of movement, and to the impression of a huge crowd:

ciegos, mudos y tullidos,	The blind, the mute and the crippled,
leprosos, febricitantes,	The lepers, the fever-ridden,
endemoniados, convulsos,	The bewitched, the convulsed,
paralíticos y orates;	The paralytic and the insane;
gentes de todas naciones	People of all nations
con diferencia de trajes,	With their difference in dress,
con diversidad de idiomas,	With their variety of languages,
con distintos ademanes.	With their different gestures.

(p. 458)

After the altercation in the temple between Aldana and the Duke of Normandy the scene shifts to Paris, to Part III, entitled "Las charlas" ("The Prattle"). This part, also written in *romance* meter could again be a candidate for inclusion in a historical ballad. It is a very cleverly put together composite view of the agitation which grips the French capital, buzzing with the news of the arrival of the Spanish gentleman come to challenge the Duke of Normandy. With a touch of irony, the narrator tells us about the rumors that swirl around this personage about to engage a French prince in a duel to the death. With the description of all this agitation, the narrator succeeds in giving heroic proportions to the figure of Aldana and in laying the groundwork for the epic encounter. Paris itself is not described in great detail, though we are told of streets, plazas, porches, workshops, taverns, and temples. There seems to be a certain ambivalence in Rivas' mind about the French capital. On the one hand he mentions the greatness to which Heaven destined it and the "Moral importance / With which it rules the World today" (p. 460). But he also calls it "The modern Babylon, / That turbulent Paris" (p. 459), full of spectacles, jokes, fights, fiestas, "Which was always the constant scene / Of the highest virtues, / Of the most horrendous vices" (p. 460).

The next two parts, entitled respectively "El salón" and "La taberna" ("The Tavern"), really set this composition apart from the ballads. They are written to a great extent in pure dramatic form and therefore contribute to give the poem a much looser structure than that of the *romances*. True, the *Romances históricos* (*Historical Ballads*) have many scenes which could be called dramatic, but with rare exceptions they are not written in pure dialogue form and are not set apart as independent dramatic units with characteristics essentially different from the rest of the work.

This is precisely what happens here. There are two self-contained dramatic episodes which give a contrasting view of what two typical segments of the Paris population—the upper class and the populace—think of the coming event. There is a good deal of realism in both sets of conversations, proving once more that the Romantic, far from being confined to a world of fantasy, is capable of giving us a realistic view of society. The contrast between the two scenes could not be greater. On the one hand a richly furnished salon where two aristocratic ladies, a widow and her daughter, are in the company of a count and an abbot, who are joined in a short while by a young baron. The conversation, whose subject is of course the challenge by the Spanish gentleman to the French duke, proceeds on a fairly genteel level, with the widow showing that upper-class ladies are not above lending an ear to all kinds of superstitious nonsense. She has heard it said, and she obviously at least half believes, that the Spaniard has made himself invulnerable and that a "detestable rabbi" has engraved on his armor words of the Scriptures.

This tendency to believe outlandish stories is what she has in common with the women of the lower class who appear in the tavern scene. One of the two women says she has heard that the Spaniard's lance had been given him by a wizard. But then, some of the other characters in this scene also seem ready to believe anything. After all, we are in the Middle Ages and the lower classes especially are prone to superstition in keeping with the times. A lackey, for instance, claims that he had heard his master say that the duel was on account of a lady who was held, enchanted, in a glass urn by a necromancer. Some of the other figures in the tavern are a butcher, a soldier, and a *matón de oficio* (a professional bully or braggart). They

have all met in a place which could not be more different from
the elegant salon of the first scene. It is a dark cellar which is
reached from a narrow and dirty street through a ramp. It
has no windows and its warped walls are covered with soot.
The author certainly does his best to present a rather negative
view of the popular milieu as opposed to the genteel settings
of the aristocratic salon. Can we read into this a class prejudice
of the by now very conservative Rivas himself? Perhaps. Be that
as it may, a dispute breaks out between the soldier and the braggart, who continues the literary tradition of the Plautine *Miles
Gloriosus* and the Spanish *Rufián* whom we meet especially in
the Spanish theater of the Renaissance.[11] The fight degenerates
into violence, and blood is spilled. The poet with visible disgust
writes of this episode: "And that repulsive cavern / Was a cave
of the devil, / A horrible pandemonium, / A picture of hell"
(p. 474).

The epic tone prevails in the next part entitled *La lid* ("The
Combat"), which describes the duel between Aldana and the
Frenchman. Here is another passage that could have formed
part of a ballad and could just as well have been written in
ballad meter. Rivas chose to write it in the *octava real*, which he
had used in *El paso honroso* (*The Passage at Arms*) and *Florinda*. The descriptive talents of Rivas are once more in the fore-
front, and the epic clash between the two enemies is rendered
with great vigor. If the dramatic scenes were static, except for
the fight in the tavern, there certainly is no lack of action
here, and we are once more forced to reject Azorín's assertion
that there is no movement in the esthetic conception of Rivas.[12]

The final part, entitled "El rescate" ("The Ransom"), is partly
in dialogue form but is essentially epic in its confrontation between Aldana and the French court. The dialogued portions are
written in the traditional *redondillas*, while the narrative portions are written in *romance* meter. We are reminded of the
romance "Un embajador español ("A Spanish Ambassador"). The
same nationalism pervades this passage. In "Un embajador
español" we had a tough Spaniard defying a French king. Here
we have a brave Spaniard, the perfect combination of religious
devotion, courage, and skill in the handling of weapons, facing
up to a group of powerful Frenchmen and with his strong per-

sonality forcing them to yield to his demand. By now we have
seen several Franco-Spanish confrontations in the works of
Rivas. It is legitimate to point out that this latest example is
again the result of a lingering resentment toward the France
against whom he fought in the Napoleonic wars.

IV   El aniversario

A.   The Plot

In the shortest of the three *leyendas*, *El aniversario* (*The
Anniversary*), the town of Badajoz is celebrating the two-
hundredth anniversary of its liberation from the Moors in 1230
and is enjoying a truce between the two factions of the
Bejaranos and the Portugaleses, who with their vicious fighting
had for a year made life in the town unbearable. But the peace
is soon broken when a young man of the Portugaleses clan,
aided by two friends, kidnaps the young and beautiful Doña
Leonor de Bejarano in the midst of the festivities after having
killed her escort. Civil war now breaks out again. A lonely
priest, assisted by a sexton, decides to celebrate Mass in spite
of the carnage. Plaintively he addresses the image of the Lord
in the deserted cathedral, asking Him why He permits the
bloodshed and why He allows His temple to remain empty on
such a solemn day. As he turns around and utters the sacred
phrase, "The Lord be with you," he sees to his horror that the
cathedral has been filled with the skeletons of the conquistadors
who had liberated Badajoz centuries before and who have
emerged from their tombs to celebrate the anniversary of the
glorious event. The priest finishes the ceremony; as he ends it
with the words, "Go, Mass is over," the ghostly visitors disappear, while the killing continues on the outside. The priest
falls to the ground dead.

B.   Analysis

Three moments make up this *leyenda,* probably based like
Maldonado on a local tradition: The fiestas commemorating the
liberation of the town, the kidnapping and the ensuing fighting,
and the Mass. The first part, written in *romance heroico* meter,

is a realistic rendering of the festivities, touched with genuine *costumbrismo;* it includes a splendid example of Rivas' virtuosity with the play of light and shadows. In the middle of the plaza a huge bonfire has been lit:

Aquel rojo esplendor la plaza llena,	That red splendor fills the square,
refleja del gran templo en las columnas,	Is reflected on the colums of the big temple,
en las lejanas torres, en las casas,	On the far-away towers, on the houses,
en los humanos rostros que circulan;	On the human faces moving about;
y si con viva luz perfila y corta	And if with a lively light it outlines
cuanto alcanza en redor, sombras oscuras	All that it reaches, it also creates Dark shadows, so vague, so fleeting,
causa también, tan vagas, tan movibles,	That it gives everything fantastic shapes. (p. 482)
que con formas fantásticas lo abulta	

There is also a masterful description of the running of a bull through the streets of Badajoz. This type of amusement is still popular today in some parts of Spain, and Rivas no doubt had witnessed such scenes himself. The ferociousness and the power of the animal are skillfully conveyed in the lines: "He runs, tramples under foot, charges, draws back, / Making the ground tremble under his hoofs" (p. 482). This bull-running has a somewhat comic moment when the mayor, out patrolling the streets at the head of a number of *alguaciles* (constables), is charged by the bull and knocked down. The aristocratic author, giving vent to his resentment of the masses exclaims: "The poor mayor took quite a fall, / Accompanied by much shouting, for the rabble, / Oh tendency typical of the lower class!, always applauds / When the one in command receives a beating" (p. 483).

This realistic, almost *costumbrista* episode contrasts with the partly dramatic passage, composed in *romance* meter, which follows and which relates the kidnapping of Doña Leonor de Bejarano. Here too Rivas displays his ability to describe the effect of light when speaking of the festival lights which combine with the light of the moon to project on the square an illumination "Now silvery, now reddish, / And such a soft brightness . . . , / That it dressed the wide plaza / In a magic appearance" (p. 484). The final moment describing the actual kidnapping of the girl and the killing of her escort is full of movement; and once more, at the risk of being repetitive, we emphasize that when action is needed in Rivas' poetry, there is no lack of it.

The final part, written in *silvas* (combining eleven- and seven-syllable lines) is a combination of lyrical, religious, and macabre elements, which form a pronounced contrast with the first two parts. It begins with a lyrical outburst on the part of the narrator, who deplores the civil war destroying Badajoz and appeals to the sun not to shed its light on the scenes of horror in the town. The religious element is represented by the lonely priest who decides to celebrate Mass, impelled to do so by the mysterious ringing of one of the cathedral bells. In the last episode, the skeletons make their appearance. In spite of the macabre aspect of this moment, a kind of epic feeling emanates from it as we are told that these are the skeletons of the erstwhile conquistadors who do not want this day to go by without paying homage to God.

V *The* Romances *and the* Leyendas

After reading the *leyendas* we must conclude that on the whole Rivas' narrative art in these compositions has not surpassed that of the *romances históricos* (*Historical Ballads*). We do note the same descriptive ability, the same flair for light and color, the same emphasis on and skillful utilization of contrast. He can still convincingly present an epic clash, such as that between Aldana and the Duke of Normandy in *Maldonado*, or an epic confrontation, such as the one between Aldana and the French court.

On the other hand, while the metrical variety shows virtuosity, we somehow miss the vigorous uniformity of the *romance* and its frequently epic air. We are touched by the candid faith so well expressed in *La azucena milagrosa* (*The Miraculous Lily*), but one of the reasons why *Maldonado* appeals more to us is that of the three *leyendas*, it is the one which in tone comes closest to the *romances*. As for *El aniversario*, it is probably the weakest of the three, mainly because its different parts—the realistic, the dramatic, and the macabre—do not mesh in a completely convincing fashion. And this is perhaps where the *romances* must be considered superior to the *leyendas*. While recognizing that Rivas' artistic powers have remained on a high level, we miss the perfectly integrated structure of the *romances*, with their magnificent tableaux and their always gripping narrative movement.

CHAPTER 7

Rivas' Later Dramas

I Rivas' New Manner in the Drama

RIVAS' first dramatic works were written according to the precepts of Neoclassic theory, the last in this series being the Moratinian comedy *Tanto vales cuanto tienes*. Then came the thunderclap of *Don Alvaro*. Rivas served notice that a Spanish writer, too, could produce a super-Romantic play in the manner of Hugo's *Hernani* and Dumas' *Antony*. But no other truly revolutionary play followed *Don Alvaro*. It was as if Rivas' dramatic super-Romanticism had exhausted itself with this drama. He remained a Romantic, as we have seen, in the *Romances históricos* (*Historical Ballads*) and the *Leyendas*, but his later plays, except *El desengaño en un sueño* (*Disillusionment in a Dream*), though containing some Romantic ingredients, cannot be considered full-fledged Romantic works. Three of them—*Solaces de un prisionero o Tres noches de Madrid* (*Relaxations of a Prisoner or Three Nights in Madrid*, published in 1841), *La morisca de Alajuar* (*The Moorish Girl from Alajuar*, 1841), and *El crisol de la lealtad* (*The Test of Loyalty*; 1842), each of which is called a *comedia* by the author—are rather echoes of the great Spanish *comedias* of the Baroque period, particularly those of Calderón, while the fourth, *El parador de Bailén* (*The Inn of Bailén;* 1844), is a Moratinian farce. The construction of the first three plays, with their three *jornadas* or acts, their themes, the salient role of the *gracioso* or comic servant in at least two of them—*Solaces de un prisionero* and *El crisol de la lealtad*—, the devices which lead to the dénouement, all remind us of Calderón.[1]

Why did Rivas not write more plays in the super-Romantic vein? Why the return to the Baroque mold in at least three of his five later dramas? We do not quite agree with Allison Peers' view that these plays indicate a lack of interest in formal drama on the part of the author and a desire to write plays mainly for relaxation "in any style that suited and came easily to him."[2] True, in a prefatory note to *Solaces de un prisionero* (*Relaxations of a Prisoner*) Rivas declared that his intention in writing this play was merely "to occupy my imagination and to give my readers and spectators a few hours of honest diversion and entertainment" and that he had followed no particular rule upon composing it.[3] But the similarity in tone between this play—and some of his other later dramas—and the drama of the seventeenth century is too striking for us to be satisfied by this explanation. Rivas was obviously aiming for a return to the Golden Age of Spanish drama. Had he not declared in his reception speech at the Spanish Academy in October, 1834, that Spaniards would see a revival of the glory of Lope de Vega, Calderón, Moreto, Alarcón, and others?[4] Besides, as Rivas was getting older, his political conservatism and nationalism were becoming increasingly strong. As a confirmed nationalist and conservative, he was bound to move away from Byronic Romanticism, as exemplified to a certain extent by *Don Alvaro*, toward more national and traditionalist forms in drama. This nationalism, which we have already seen in the *Romances históricos* (*Historical Ballads*), was present in Rivas' theater beginning in 1840; it was expressed in plays that were clearly aimed at awakening memories of Spain's greatest dramatic period.

II *Miscellaneous Plays*

A. *Solaces de un prisionero*

Notwithstanding his disclaimer, Rivas obviously composed *Solaces de un prisionero* with one eye on his august seventeenth-century predecessors. As in a Baroque cape-and-sword *comedia*[5] we have here gentlemen with their faces muffled, going through the streets of Madrid accompanied by their servants. Ladies are courted by these same gentlemen, the latter meeting in the dark and fighting with their swords. Moreover, the servants with their remarks and actions provide comic relief and generally fill the role of the traditional *graciosos*. The play is divided

into three acts, and while, as the title indicates, the action develops over a period of time not much greater than in Neoclassic
comedy, there is—as in so many Golden Age plays—a constant
change of scenery: From a street, to a room in a house, to a
garden, to the royal palace in Madrid, and so on.

The plot is actually quite simple. The French king Francis I,
a prisoner of Emperor Charles V in Madrid after the battle of
Pavia (1525), escapes each night through a hole in his apart-
ment's wall and courts Doña Leonor, who does not know his
true identity. It so happens that the Emperor is wooing the
cousin of Leonor, who lives in the same house as the latter; he
finds out that his prisoner is roaming the streets of Madrid at
night and traps him finally in Doña Leonor's house; but Charles
is generous and forgiving to Francis since peace between France
and Spain has already been arranged and needs only the French
king's signature to go into effect.

Both sovereigns are models of nobility of character, and it
is emphasized that in spite of his amorous escapades Francis has
not broken his word to the Emperor not to escape from Madrid.
Thus the element of honor, so dear to Baroque playwrights, is
also given great importance. One of the last touches of the
play also makes us think of the seventeenth-century productions:
Doña Leonor, who at the end discovers the true identity of her
suitor, and who realizes that marriage is out of the question,
decides to enter a convent and expresses the point of view, so
often seen in Baroque literature, that "este mundo es todo
engaños" (this world is all deceit).[6]

While much of the atmosphere of the Golden Age plays is
thus recreated, there is nevertheless a marked difference between
Solaces de un prisionero and Baroque drama, and that is in the
language. This play has none of the metaphoric density and
the frequent obscurity of the works of Lope de Vega, Calderón,
and their disciples. It is written mostly in the traditional eight-
syllable verse; there are images of course, but the language is
fairly straightforward. There is no concerted effort to repro-
duce the speech of the Golden Age. Only now and then do we
hear expressions which could have been uttered by characters
out of Lope's and Calderón's plays. Such is the case of *hacer
terrero*, or court a lady from the street (p. 366), or the line

"¿Qué os hiela? ¿Qué os petrifica?" (What amazes you? What petrifies you? (p. 416), which is similar to the line occasionally found in Golden Age drama: "¿Qué os admira? ¿Qué os espanta?" (What surprises you? What frightens you?).

While not a great play, *Solaces de un prisionero* is interesting especially as an attempt to create a *comedia* in the Baroque manner. It is entertaining enough and fulfills the avowed aim of the author to provide the reader or spectator with a few hours of diversion.

B. *La morisca de Alajuar*

The historical background of this play is the expulsion of the Moslem *moriscos* from Spain in 1609. The publication of the decree of expulsion coincides with a *morisco* uprising in the mountains near Valencia, led by Mulim-Albenzar, whose daughter María has been raised as a Christian by her wet-nurse, the Catholic Felisa. Mulim-Albenzar is killed by Spanish soldiers, and María is taken prisoner. She is freed by her lover, Don Fernando, a Castilian nobleman, son of a grandee, the Count of Salazar, who is in charge of the expulsion operation and who is unaware of his son's love for María. To free his beloved, Fernando has had to kill a Spanish captain who had tried to rape her. He flees with the girl and is married to her by a priest. But they are arrested and brought back to Valencia, where they are to die on the scaffold, according to an order signed by the Count of Salazar and two other Castilian officials, the *Comendador* (Knight-Commander of a military order) and the Marquis of Caracena. Before the execution, however, the count discovers that the condemned young man is his son and had killed only to protect María's honor. The Marquis learns that María is actually his daughter, whom he had abandoned as a baby in the hands of the Christian Felisa. The latter, fearing the wrath of Mulim-Albenzar, of whose child she had also been in charge, had substituted the Christian baby for the Moorish child when it had died in a fall and had deceived the Moorish chieftain into believing that the new child was his. Thus Fernando has actually married not the daughter of Mulim-Albenzar but a girl of Christian blood. The play ends with both parents giving their blessing to the marriage.

In *La morisca de Alajuar*, as in *Solaces de un prisionero*, Rivas
caught something of the form and the spirit of the seventeenth-
century *comedia*. There are the three *jornadas* or acts, there are
many characters—fifteen in all—, frequent changes in scenery,
and a servant who, though not a true *gracioso* like Pierres in
Solaces, does help his master Don Fernando and to a certain
extent act as his advisor. The fairly complex plot, involving lovers
of apparently different ethnic backgrounds, their trials and
tribulations, and the final surprising revelations about María's
origin, has Romantic elements, but could also have been devised
by Lope de Vega or Calderón. The fierce antagonisms between
Moslems and Christians and the intolerance of the latter, well
personified by the inflexible Count Salazar, also tend to make
us think of the drama of the seventeenth century, in which
loyalty to Church and king is so often an essential element.

Rivas seems to be somewhat ambivalent on the question of
Christian versus Moslem. On the one hand there is an underlying intimation that Christianity is superior to Islam and that
the *moriscos*, as sworn enemies of Christian Spain, had to be
crushed. Yet there also seems to be indirect condemnation of
the inflexibility of the Count of Salazar, who is shown as the
incarnation of intolerance. Furthermore, Rivas is fairly objective in presenting the dissatisfaction of the Moslems with their
status in Spain. Their resentment is given an air of legitimacy.
There is strong intimation of this in the following exclamation
of a Moslem: "... Tomorrow they will come / ... Those who
will steal our possessions, / Soil our reputation / And our honor
in the persons / Of our daughters, wives, and sisters; / Those
who will tear away from us together with our souls / Our sweet
children" (p. 436). And Mulim-Albenzar exclaims at one point:
"Today the Moorish nation / Will avenge all the oppression /
Which the Christian has imposed upon it" (p. 441).

As for the language it is, as in *Solaces*, much simpler and more
direct than in the Baroque drama. Only now and then are there
echoes of the style of the Golden Age. One such example occurs
when Corbacho finds his master Fernando, who had fallen
from a horse, in the arms of María. Corbacho exclaims: "When I
thought I would find you / At the foot of a rough crag, /
Smashed in two thousand pieces / Turning the streams / Into

foamy carmine, / And the emerald grass / Into corals and rubies, / I find you, God bless you, / . . . Sitting on painted flowers / And in the arms of a seraph" (p. 429).

C. *El crisol de la lealtad* (*The Test of Loyalty*)

This is another attempt on Rivas's part to write a play in the Golden Age manner. The first of the three *jornadas*, which is a skillful exposition of the basic problems of the *comedia*, promises more than the author actually delivers in the balance of the play. One of the reasons is perhaps the lack of unity of action. The attention of the reader is divided by two parallel developments: An impostor, Don Lope de Azagra, counseled by the wicked monk Mauricio, claims he is King Alfonso el Batallador of Aragón (1104–34), long presumed dead in the battle of Fraga. At the same time Don Pedro López de Azagra, son of the impostor, is in love with Isabel Torrellas, daughter of one of the Aragonese noblemen whose support the impostor has succeeded in enlisting, and is loved in turn by the present queen of Aragón. This love triangle, which reminds us of a similar situation in Guillén de Castro's seventeenth-century *Las mocedades del Cid* (*The Feats of the Young Cid*), prevents us from focusing our attention on the more interesting dramatic line, that of Don Lope de Azagra and his attempt at seizing the throne of Aragón.

After a series of rather implausible developments, the impostor, who has failed to carry out his scheme, dies of grief and old age. His son Pedro, who has been torn between loyalty to the Queen and love for his father, and who has killed the evil Mauricio, receives permission from the sovereign to marry Isabel but decides to postpone the marriage for a year and to wash away in the struggle against Islam the stain on his family honor. The intense conflict in the soul of Don Lope between his ambition and his remorse for the role he is playing is well brought out, especially in the first scene of the first *jornada*, when the old man exclaims at one point: "Sí, concluiré la carrera; / Sí, saciaré mi ambición; / Pero un noble corazón / Tiene la voz muy severa" ("Yes, I will go to the end of the road; / I will satiate my ambition; / But a noble heart / Has a very severe voice").[7] In the last scene of the play the intensity of his grief, culminating in his death in his son's arms, is also convincingly rendered. We wish, however, that the author had gone more deeply into the problems created by Lope's plans and into the mechanism of his ultimate failure.

Mauricio, his adviser, is suitably evil, though a greater complexity of character would have been desirable. He is introduced as a Benedictine monk, but his true status is somewhat ambiguous. When Don Lope is about to die, Mauricio says to himself: "Since I am reputed to be a clergyman, / It is important for me to impress upon everyone that I am one indeed / So that I may perhaps delay / Or avoid my punishment" (p. 58). We could therefore conclude that Mauricio is a false monk who had donned the ecclesiastic garb to better carry out his nefarious scheme. At any rate it would be surprising if the by now conservative Duke had meant to ascribe the role of blackhearted villain to a genuine monk.

It is interesting to note that of all Rivas' plays this is the one where the *gracioso* has the most important role.[8] The swineherd Berrio, who plays this part, reminds us more of the coarse and grotesque *bobos* (fools) of the Spanish Renaissance drama than of the more sophisticated *graciosos* of the Baroque period. Berrio is stupid, ignorant, a coward, and a glutton. But he also promotes the action as he exchanges garbs with Pedro (kept a prisoner in his father's fortress), to allow him to escape.

The play has the usual variety of meters: octosyllables, hendecasyllables, heptasyllables, and even some pentasyllables. The language is usually clear and rather devoid of images. Now and then we are reminded of the mode of expression dear to the Golden Age, as in the following lines in which Pedro alludes to Isabel's tears: "¿Por qué a tu mustio semblante / Dan sin luz los bellos ojos / Esas perlas por despojos? . . ." ("Why do your beautiful eyes deprived of light / Give those pearls as booty / To your sad countenance? . . ." p. 15).

D. *El parador de Bailén* (*The Inn of Bailén*)

This comedy in three acts follows the Neoclassic precepts of unity of place—the action takes place in a patio of the inn— and time—the action begins at three in the afternoon and ends at dawn on the following day—, as well as that of action. But it is essentially a farce, all the more since the moralizing element, so important in the Neoclassic comedy, is not as clearly presented here as in some other Neoclassic plays. A didactic purpose may be seen to some extent in the fact that a young girl escapes marriage to a fool and marries the man she loves.

A ridiculous character, Don Lesmes, who is to marry the heroine, Doña Clara, against her will, becomes drunk and is put away in a chest. Later on he slips into the same chest with an elderly widow, Doña Genoveva, whom he takes in the darkness to be a young girl. A young officer, Don Fernando, in love with Doña Clara, changes clothes with the addle-brained fiancé in order to palm him off on the ridiculous widow, who is in love with Don Fernando. The officer then struggles with a servant, the latter believing that his love—actually Doña Clara disguised as the servant girl—is about to run away with the young officer. Everything ends well when the father of the girl, Don Luis, becomes convinced that Don Lesmes is far from the ideal son-in-law and agrees to the marriage of his daughter and Don Fernando.

Although there are many differences between the two plays, this amiable farce reminds one of the comedy *El sí de las niñas* (*Girls' Consent*, 1806) by Leandro Fernández de Moratín. In *El sí de las niñas* the heroine is also to be married against her will, in this case to the uncle of the man she loves. The young man in the play is also a soldier, and the action again takes place in an inn. Everything ends well, with the young man and the girl marrying with the blessing of the uncle. There the resemblance ends, but these common elements give some impression that Rivas may have written *El parador de Bailén*, perhaps unconsciously, parodying *El sí de las niñas*. At any rate he succeeds in making us laugh, especially at the ridiculous old lady Doña Genoveva, who pursues in vain the young Don Fernando.

III El desengaño en un sueño

A. General Observations

Most of the dramas and tragedies of Rivas deal with a certain action set against a historical background. Even in *Don*

Alvaro part of the action develops against the backdrop of the
eighteenth-century War of the Austrian Succession. In the four
acts of *El desengaño en un sueño* (*Disillusionment in a Dream*;
1844) on the other hand, a play called a "fantastic drama" by
the author, everything is fictitious and fantastic. At the same
time, however, the play is richer in ideas than any of Rivas'
other dramatic productions.

The play, which had to wait thirty-three years for a performance, was Rivas' favorite dramatic creation. In this special
affection for *El desengaño en un sueño* he was not alone. A
number of nineteenth-century critics acclaimed it. Cañete called
it "the most original and lofty poetic work of our author."[9] For
Cueto it was a "magnificent fantastic legend,"[10] and the playwright Juan Eugenio Hartzenbusch, in his preface to the fifth
volume of the 1854–55 edition of Rivas' collected works, considered it and *Don Alvaro* two of the best dramas of the first
half of the nineteenth century. Even in this century Allison
Peers declared it the first of Rivas' dramatic productions after
Don Alvaro and wrote that it is in some respects superior to
the latter.[11]

B. Plot

An old man, Marcolán, who has magic powers, and his son
Lisardo live on a desert island, for Marcolán wants to protect
Lisardo from the troubled life which the stars have in store
for him if he should venture forth into the world. Lisardo wants
to break the bonds of isolation and get to know the world, which
will perhaps give him love, wealth, power, glory, and fame. The
old man finally agrees to his leaving, but before Lisardo is to
depart he puts him to sleep and in his dream, with the help
of celestial and infernal spirits, he causes him to go through a
number of worldly experiences.

First Lisardo meets pure love personified by the sweet Zora,
whom he marries. Then he acquires wealth, which he enjoys
in a magnificent palace. But fanned by the voice of the spirit
of evil, the suspicion that his new-found friends covet his wife
and his wealth gives him some anxious moments. The voice
of the spirit of evil suggests to Lisardo that he must reach out

for power, since power is the "amparo de la belleza, / defensor de la riqueza" ("Protector of beauty, / Defender of wealth"). Thus Lisardo becomes a general, highly esteemed by the king and queen of the realm. But the spirit of evil is relentless: It is not sufficient to be a victorious general. Why not be king and why not acquire possession of the beautiful queen? The Queen manifests her love for the general, and he reciprocates her feelings. The sweet Zora is rejected and departs heart-broken; and at the prodding of the Queen, Lisardo murders the King.

Now king himself and married to the Queen, Lisardo should be happy. But he is weighed down by remorse for his crime and thinks the King's blood has left a stain on his hand that cannot be washed away. While hunting in the woods he comes upon a witch, who suggests that his future is dark and gives him a ring which will permit him to be invisible. Thanks to the ring he is able to listen unseen to a conversation between the Queen and his friend Arbolán and hear his wife plan to poison him because she loves Arbolán. In the meantime the people have turned against him, and his efforts to have the Queen arrested are unavailing, for Arbolán informs Lisardo's guards that Lisardo had murdered the former king. Thanks to the ring of the witch Lisardo is able to escape.

But his tribulations are not ended. Finding himself once more in the garden where he had first met Zora, he learns that she is dead and about to be buried. Zora's father informs him that he, Lisardo, has lost everything he possessed. Lisardo then calls on the power of hell to help him. The devil appears and furnishes him with a sword and a group of bandits so that he may regain power. But a bronze wall, on top of which stands an angel with a flaming sword in each hand, suddenly bars their way, and the bandits as well as the devil disappear. Lisardo is finally captured by his enemies and is shortly to be executed. After vain attempts, while in jail, to recapture the allegiance of the people and after seeing the specters of the King and Zora, Lisardo expresses the wish to be back with his father. Marcolán then puts an end to the dream and Lisardo awakens. He has learned his lesson and declares he will never leave his father.

C. Sources and Influences

There are many elements reminiscent of native and foreign works in *El desengaño en un sueño*. As Peers points out, the idea of teaching a moral lesson by means of a dream is of Oriental origin.[12] One of its first expressions in Spanish is a story found in the *Conde Lucanor*, written by the fourteenth-century prose writer Juan Manuel. However, it bears practically no resemblance to Rivas' play. There are some echoes of Calderón's *La vida es sueño* (*Life Is a Dream*). In Calderón's play a father makes a prisoner of his son to thwart the power of the stars, which have forecast that one day his son will humble him. The speech of Lisardo at the beginning of *El desengaño*, in which he complains about his confinement to the island, makes us think of the lines of *La vida es sueño*'s protagonist, Segismundo, in which he laments the fact that as a prisoner in his tower, and in spite of the fact that he is a man, he has less freedom than animals (Act I, sc. 2). And the following line of Lisardo: "¡Mísera condición en que nacemos!" ("Into what a miserable state we are born!"; p. 101) reminds us of Segismundo's exclamation in *La vida es sueño*: "... el delito mayor / del hombre es haber nacido" ("Man's greatest crime is to have been born," Act I, sc. 2). But the similarity with *La vida es sueño* ends here, for *El desengaño* develops in a way quite different from that of Calderón's masterpiece.

The likeliest Spanish source, however, is a certain *comedia de magia* (play of magic)—a genre that had been popular in Spain for a century—entitled *Sueños hay que lecciones son, o Efectos del desengaño* (*There Are Dreams Which Are Lessons, or the Effects of Disillusionment*), which appeared in the early years of the nineteenth century and was an adaptation of an earlier play by a D. M. A. Igual.[13] There is here, too, a young man put to sleep so that he will experience what the world has to offer. After his unhappy experiences he awakens and decides not to abandon his family. Though *Sueños hay* may very well have been the basis for Rivas' play, he embellished the original considerably with his own talents and perhaps by some borrowings from English literature.[14]

Rivas had probably also read *The Tempest*, *Macbeth*, and

Hamlet. There are elements from all three works in *El desengaño*. As in *El desengaño*, the setting of *The Tempest* is a lonely island, where Prospero, a magician, lives with his daughter Miranda. Prospero's magical powers, like those of Marcolán, control the action of the play. Other similarities have been pointed out by Peers,[15] who has also discussed *Hamlet's* contributions.[16] Finally, the Queen's prodding of Lisardo before the murder of the King and other details such as the imagined bloodstain are definitely suggestive of *Macbeth*.[17]

In their discussion of possible influences neither Peers nor Boussagol mention the drama *Der Traum ein Leben* (*A Life in a Dream*) by the Austrian playwright Franz Grillparzer, which also bears a striking similarity to *El desengaño*. It was performed for the first time in 1834 in Vienna and appeared in print in 1840. In this play, as in *El desengaño*, a young man wants to gain wealth, fame, and power. The night before he is to leave his father, he has dream experiences showing his fate if he goes out into the world. He rejects the love of a girl in order to achieve his aim and obtains a crown through murder and marriage. He is toppled from the throne and awakens when his situation is at its most distressful.

Rivas did not know German and thus could not have read the play in the original. *El desengaño* was completed before August 20, 1842, and as Richard B. O'Connell points out, the period between 1840 and August 20, 1842 "is much too short for a French or a Spanish translation of the Austrian play to have appeared and been read by Rivas."[18] May we then suppose that Rivas had a friend in Vienna who sent him an account of the play? This is a possibility but only a remote possibility. It is much more likely that Grillparzer modeled his plot upon *Sueños hay*, the same play which probably served as a basis for *El desengaño*. "The Austrian writer read not only the masterpieces of the Golden Age but any Spanish play he could find."[19] Thus it is not at all far-fetched to assume that Grillparzer read *Sueños hay* and utilized its plot for his own *Der Traum ein Leben*.[20]

D. The Meaning of the Play

As Rupert C. Allen has noted, *El desengaño en un sueño* is "a mythic play dramatizing the psychological transformation of a young man."[21] It is mythic because it "is a story about issues so fundamental to the conditions of human existence that it can be expressed only by means of elementary symbols and archetypal figures which transcend the accidents of time and place."[22] To be more specific, we might add that Lisardo symbolizes man and his quest for love, wealth, and power. This quest develops through contact with essentially mythical archetypes. The first of these is Zora, a projection of Lisardo's erotic ideal, who incarnates the possibility of happy union between man and woman, and whom Lisardo will reject in his drive for self-aggrandizement. We then meet Arbolán, Lisardo's antagonist, who can be said to represent the great rival of man in his quest. The next important figures are the King and Queen, who represent "the transpersonal Father and Mother principles in Divine Marriage."[23] Lisardo, prodded by the spirit of evil, a sort of embodiment of his ego drive, decides to destroy this union and to take the Queen for himself; here his real troubles begin. Both the Queen, separated from the King, and the witch are to a certain extent incarnations of the forces of darkness who assert their power over him. Lisardo sinks further into distress, and even the devil, the supreme embodiment of the forces of darkness, cannot help him.

It then seems that through this mythic play Rivas wants to convey the message that in this world, man is driven by a thirst for wealth and power, which more often than not proves stronger than love. But even when acquired, wealth and power do not ensure happiness. Power often causes man to become involved in crimes: "¡Oh ambición! ... ¡Oh poderío! / ¿Quién con vos no es criminal?" ("Oh ambition! ... Oh power! / Who with you is not a criminal?; p. 114). What then is the solution? Perhaps a quiet, secluded life, away from the torments of the world. The idea is not original, for this is essentially the *beatus ille* theme of Horace frequently found in Spanish literature.[24]

Rupert C. Allen sees Marcolán's role as essentially negative and the conclusion of the play as ironical. According to this point of view, what the old Marcolán has done is what psychologists call "patriarchal castration." He has castrated his son spiritually by keeping him a prisoner on the desert island, not allowing him to develop his potential. In other words he has brought about the downfall of his son's "ego-consciousness."[25] To prove that Rivas was conscious of the irony, Allen adduces the link between the names Marcolán and Arbolán, formed by adding the suffix –*án* to the words *márcola* (pruning hook) and *árbol* (tree).[26] Thus it turns out that Mr. "Pruning Hook" has prevented the free development of the young tree, at the same time creating through his son's psyche the figure of a superior tree which in the final analysis crushes Lisardo.

There is a slight flaw in Allen's argument. He makes it appear too much as if Marcolán were driven from the start by a desire to keep possession of his son and hence to castrate him psychologically. He does not mention the star motif, Rivas' starting point for his play. It is Marcolán's fear of what the stars have in store for Lisardo which prompts his actions. On the other hand it can be argued that if Marcolán's initial impulse was to protect his son, *in the process* of saving him he clips his wings and crushes his ego-consciousness as effectively as if his primary intention had been to bring about this result.

With this slight correction we can accept Allen's theory. We do not really run up against a contradiction, as might appear at first sight. It might seem that Rivas praises the secluded life while looking askance at the final result of Marcolán's magic. But Rivas might answer that psychological castration, while not desirable, is the price of a truly peaceful existence.

E. Romantic Aspects

While in *Solaces de un prisionero, La morisca de Alajuar, El crisol de la lealtad,* and of course *El parador de Bailén,* Romantic elements are manifest only to a minimal degree, they are considerably more accentuated in *Disillusionment in a Dream.* The protagonist Lisardo comes much closer to the figure of the Romantic hero than any important personages of the above-mentioned plays. Lisardo in his quest can be seen as the hero

out to overcome the cosmic forces of the universe and to make
for himself a prominent place in the sun. In his struggle with
the world he is crushed in the end, but not without putting
up a tremendous fight. And until close to the end of his worldly
experiences he remains defiant. Even in his prison, when all
seems lost, he feels himself strong enough to try again if he
could only free himself:

Sí, saludable lección,	Yes, [it is] a salutary lesson,
que me dice: del dominio	Which tells me: Blood and
la sangre y el exterminio	extermination
las firmes columnas son.	Are the firm columns of rule.
La sangre de los traidores,	The blood of the traitors,
el exterminio total	The total elimination
de todo osado rival,	Of all daring rivals,
son sus cimientos mejores.	Are its best foundations.
Si lograran mis furores,	If my fury,
si mi sañuda altivez	If my furious pride
de esta torre la estrechez	Succeeded in shaking off
burlar . . .	The narrowness of this tower . . .
¡Ah! . . .Por vida mía,	Oh! . . . On my life,
que el mundo no me vería	The world would not see me
cual estoy, segunda vez.	A second time the way I am.
	(pp. 112–13)

And shortly afterward he exclaims:

If I only succeeded in
Going out into the world once more,
Who would be able to resist
My vengeful rancor?
With what furious pleasure . . .
Would I inundate it in blood
And drown it in terror! (p. 114)

In Lisardo's meeting with the witch, though he finally cowers
before her when she threatens to divulge his crime, he addresses
her proudly in the manner of the most Romantic rebel: "Si tú
del hondo aterrador infierno / osas la frente alzar, / sírvate de
gobierno / que nunca, nunca yo supe temblar" ("If you dare
to raise your face / Up from deep, frightful hell, / Keep in
mind /That I have never, never known how to tremble"; p. 94).

The Romantic hero is often tormented by melancholy and by doubt, and Lisardo suffers from these afflictions a number of times in the play. In this way Rivas, far from letting his hero stand as a mere symbol, imparts to him a highly human dimension. When Lisardo contemplates the possibility of ascending the throne he exclaims: "Before me, oh heavens!, a barrier arises ..., / Oh, how much higher it is / Than what my delirium gave me to understand!" (p. 83). When he is about to reject Zora's love he says: "Zora! ... So pure ..., so beautiful ..., / So tender and angelical ... / Heavens, what a mortal anguish!" (p. 87). Once on the throne Lisardo asks the question: "Who can tear me away from here?", and as the voice of the spirit of evil whispers to him: "The dagger of a murderer," Lisardo cries out: "Heavens! ... What horrible idea confounds me suddenly? / Oh!, my proud forehead / Has been struck by a frightful thunderbolt!" (p. 90).

Perhaps the most self-searching monologue is found in Act III, scene 2, when Lisardo reflects on his situation. In spite of his power he is deeply unhappy. He feels the weight of his crime on his conscience, and he laments the fact that he owes the throne to a woman. Among these gloomy thoughts of the Romantic protagonist, who seems to sense incipient failure amidst all the outward manifestations of his successful climb to power, we note the following lines:

¿Por qué no nací rey? ... Advenedizo	Why was I not born king? Those who acclaim me
tal vez con risa de desdén me llaman	Call me perhaps an upstart With a disdainful laughter in
allá en su corazón los que me aclaman. ...	their hearts. ... And their applause satisfied my
¡Y su aplauso mi orgullo satisfizo!	pride!
El mortal, ¡ay de mí!, más desdichado	I am, woe is me, the unhappiest mortal
soy que cobija con su manto el cielo,	Whom Heaven covers with its mantle,
corriendo de un anhelo en otro anhelo	Running from one desire to the next,
a una sima sin fondo despeñado.	Hurled into a bottomless pit.

(p. 93)

We have seen the importance which Rivas assigned to fate in
Don Alvaro. Here, too, the hero feels himself driven along by
an inexorable destiny. From the very beginning, fate plays an
important part with Marcolán's disclosure that the stars have
foretold a stormy future for his son; and from the very beginning fate is perceived by Lisardo as ruling supreme. Time and
again destiny is mentioned. In the first scene Lisardo exclaims,
referring to the island on which he is confined: "It is, oh
impious destiny!, / A narrow prison of my burning vigor" (p. 62).
In the same scene, the young man asks why he has been given
a forceful soul if his destiny is to live out his life in confinement. After usurping the throne Lisardo informs the Queen
that destiny had put the burden of rule on his shoulders. After
he overhears the Queen and Arbolán plotting against him he
exclaims in one of his monologues: "Is it men's horrible destiny /
To be criminals? . . ." (p. 101). Over Zora's body he moans:
"And I, I, oh impious star!, / Have killed you" (p. 107). Toward
the end destiny is mentioned a number of times. In his prison, for
instance, Lisardo asks: "What awaits me, oh cruel fate?" (p. 115).

Lisardo, the Romantic protagonist, falls in love with and
marries Zora, typical angel-woman of Romantic tradition. "Angel
celestial" (Celestial angel) Lisardo calls her in Act I, scene 2.
She is the virtuous woman, loving the simple things in life,
ready to give all her affection to her husband; she does not
care for wealth and power. In a sense she symbolizes the
secluded life Marcolán plans for his son. "Are you not enchanted / By this tranquillity, this happiness?", she asks her
husband (p. 70). Once in the palace she says: "I, as in the
garden, / Am happy in this palace, / Since here as there, / I can
call myself your dear wife" (p. 72). But the angel-woman Zora
falls victim to Lisardo's ambition. After he is made a general,
Zora tries to win him back, but to no avail. Zora announces
that she is leaving him with a broken heart. Even then Lisardo
recognizes her angelical character: "tan tierna y angelical" ("so
tender and angelical"), he exclaims (p. 87). With Romantic
resignation Zora, unfortunate victim of driving ambition, is
ready to step aside:

What a mortal poison
You give to my torn soul!
Be happy, Lisardo.
And if my death is necessary
To see you happy,
Ungrateful and fierce husband,
Your wish will be fulfilled. (p. 88)

Zora, who provides strong contrast with the scheming, treacherous Queen, dies of grief; the scene in which Lisardo finds her body is highly Romantic. He takes her out of her casket and carries her in his arms. "My angel, awaken," he cries out. "Arise, look, / Live, breathe, / Hear my voice" (p. 107). We are reminded of the *Noches lúgubres* (*Lugubrious Nights*) by the eighteenth-century writer José Cadalso, in which a bereaved lover tries to disinter the body of his dead mistress.

Other Romantic elements are the vagueness and mistiness of the dream scenes, the colorful action on the stage, the elaborateness and constant change of scenery, and the metrical variety. This last includes the *romance* meter, hendecasyllables, heptasyllables, and shorter lines, used to good effect by the spirit of evil, whose pronouncements thus acquire conciseness, making them all the more effective, as in the following case: "Es achechada / la belleza. / Es codiciada / la riqueza" ("Beauty is in danger of being ambushed. / Wealth is coveted"; p. 74).

The language of the play is simple and straightforward, with few images but some impressive lyrical bursts, especially in the second scene of Act I, in which Lisardo meets Zora. The following lines are a typical example:

Mi encanto, mi único bien,
mi tesoro, mi alegría . . .
¡Oh lumbre del alma mía!,
no miedo, lástima ten
de mi amorosa agonía . . .
Para ti sólo respiro,
y sin ti quiero la muerte.
¿Qué es vivir sin poseerte?

My delight, my only love,
My treasure, my happiness . . .
Oh light of my soul!,
Do not be afraid, pity
My amorous agony . . .
I only breathe for you,
And without you I want death.
What is life without possessing you? (p. 67)

In sum, *El desengaño en un sueño* is Rivas' most ambitious play and, we might say, one of his most interesting.

CHAPTER 8

Later Lyrics and Prose

I Lyrics

ALTHOUGH Rivas' lyric productions must take second place to his narrative poetry, he does have some interesting compositions from his younger period, among which "El faro de Malta" ("The Lighthouse of Malta") stands out. His later years produced nothing so outstanding as this piece, although several poems attract our attention. We notice for instance the moving *Lucía*, written in 1838 in stanzas of five hendecasyllables, ending in the returning leitmotif, the five syllable line "¡Pobre Lucía!" ("Poor Lucía"). It is the story of a girl pure in heart who falls victim to the lure of false love and dies as a result. As in a number of compositions of Espronceda, the Romantic view of a world where unhappiness follows happiness in seemingly inexorable fashion prevails,[1] and the transformation of happy dreams into martyrdom is emphasized. Something of that Romantic pessimism, not too common in Spanish Romanticism, is present here. The following stanza with its two metaphors, one at the beginning and the other at the end, is particularly moving: "And the flowers turned into sterile thistles, / And the sweet pleasures into martyrdom, / Delirium into horrible realities, / Love into treason and vile deceit, / And fleeting day into horrendous night."[2]

"La asonada" ("The Mob Attack"), written in Seville in 1840, while artistically less valuable, is interesting in that it shows the political posture of the ex-liberal who has turned quite conservative due to upheavals in Spain. The mob shouting "Liberty" is seen as a dangerous and detestable element when in its revolutionary ardor it is unleashed on society, and in the words of the poet deserves "only ignominious chains and the whip" (p. 521).

150

Quite Romantic is the composition entitled "No hay reparación" ("There Is No Reparation"), written in 1844. An unfaithful wife, bathed in tears and carrying flowers, hurries to the grave of her husband whose death she precipitated through her infidelity. She intends to make amends for the terrible wrong she has caused. But suddenly the ghost of her husband rises above his tomb and tells her that it is too late for tears and flowers and that she must leave: "There is no love here, / Nor do flowers give off any aroma" (p. 525). The next morning the woman is found dead next to the gravestone. The poem ends with the question: "Was it because of repentance · terror?" (p. 525). The setting of the composition, the grave, is highly Romantic and so is the ghost of the dead husband, a "White form of mist and vapor, / With two phosphorescent eyes... / Giving off a sinister glow" (p. 524). Thus the element of terror finds its culmination with the death of the woman. Although the poem is not, strictly speaking, a lyrical composition, we sense throughout it that the author expresses his own feelings about the wife's unfaithfulness through the words of the dead husband.

The poem "Desconsuelo" ("Disconsolateness") was written in Naples in 1845. Rivas was fifty-four years old by then and felt the passing of his youth keenly. His melancholy is convincingly projected in this essentially metaphoric composition, which shows us the narrator leaving behind the forest of youth and moving along the icy, dead countryside leading to the desert of old age. Suddenly he comes upon a beautiful flower and feels himself filled with the hope of recapturing his youth. But destiny keeps prodding him to move on, and in order to take the flower with him he plucks it. Alas, at this very moment it withers in his hands, and he is forced to continue on his way. The meaning of the poem is conveyed in the final two stanzas, which tell us that once you are on the way to old age an illusion of happiness "Passes like a light fire, / And destroys the heart, / Which follows it blindly" (p. 534). While it is not a very profound composition, and while the poet basically expresses a disillusionment caused by approaching old age, we sense something of the Romantic pessimism not often found in Spanish poetry, except in a few figures like Espronceda. The felicitous metaphoric structure of the forest, the desert, the dead countryside, and the flower convey forcefully the narrator's "disconsolateness."

Disillusionment with old age is also expressed in the poem "La vejez" ("Old Age"), written in Naples in 1847. The theme is indicated by the refrain, repeated throughout the composition: "Let ardent youth look / At pleasures, glory, applause, and happiness; / And old age, at vexations, discouragement, / And death, and afterward the coffin" (p. 541). This rather long piece shows some metrical variety. Hendecasyllables alternate with heptasyllables and there are also lines of five syllables. The narrator constantly contrasts the feelings and pleasures of youth with his own decrepit self. Observing a way of life that is no longer his, his inability to bridge the gap created by age gives this composition its plaintive, moving tone. The poem, in spite of its pessimism, ends on a traditionally consoling note, which reminds us of the advice of many Spanish writers of the Golden Age: While time dissolves man's strength and this world is only a stopping place, man should have faith in God and not fear death.

II *Prose*

Rivas' most ambitious prose work is the *Sublevación de Nápoles, capitaneada por Masaniello* (*The Revolt of Naples, Led by Masaniello*), which he wrote in Naples and for which he did much research.[3] It is a history of the uprising of 1647 against Spanish rule, when Naples was still part of the Spanish empire, an uprising which began as an explosion of local grievances over taxation and ended as a movement for independence crushed by the Spaniards in April, 1648. Rivas was not a professional historian, but he succeeds in presenting an interesting account of this movement. It is, however, history in the manner of many nineteenth-century historians, who were wont to concentrate on personalities and military events and ignore the deeper, underlying causes and the meaning of the events they discussed. Thus Rivas pays painstaking attention to the important figures which emerged during the uprising, especially to the strange Masaniello, and to the many military clashes and atrocities in and around Naples. But although he is aware of the various social segments in the Neapolitan population during the revolt, he does not give us a sufficiently clear picture of the aspirations, motivations, and interrelations of these classes.

Rivas writes vigorously, with well-balanced sentences and occasional bursts of brilliance in his narrative. In the following passage we sense that it is the poet rather than the historian who is writing:

The smoke of the flames of the voracious fires which, set by a frenzied crowd, devoured in a few instants immense resources, notified the unhappy families who, having taken refuge at Castelnovo, looked from its battlements onto the part of the town where their houses were, that they were already the victims of popular rage and that they were falling from the summit of opulence into the abyss of poverty and depression.[4]

There is considerable irony and narrative skill in the concise account of the visit of the French Duke of Guise, who took charge of the uprising, to the popular leader Annese in his modest abode:

[The Duke] embraced many times the harquebusier, caressed the cook, praised the free lodging and the frugal meal, conferred intimately with the generalissimo, endeavoring to eliminate in him any suspicion of being supplanted, and even acceded to going to bed with the stinking popular chieftain, spending the night at his side on a mattress on the floor, while the lady of the castle snored on another one next to theirs. (p. 248)

After his return to Spain, Rivas did not lose interest in the history of the land across the Mediterranean, and in 1854 he completed a short historical study of the Kingdom of the two Sicilies entitled *Breve reseña de la historia del Reino de las Dos Sicilias* (*Brief Narration of the Historical Development of the Kingdom of the Two Sicilies*). Here again the author displayed his erudition but due to the form of the study could not really fully bring into play his gift as a narrator.

Of greater interest for us are his two Neapolitan sketches of 1844; they deal with two excursions, one to the top of Mount Vesuvius and the other to the ruins of Paestum. The "Viaje al Vesubio" ("Journey to Vesuvius") is the more interesting of the two. It is more than the narration of a journey, for in it Rivas, aside from giving us historical information of the activities of the volcano throughout the ages, provides us with a fascinating glimpse of the crater and a description of the countryside at the foot of the mountain such as only a poet and a painter could have given us. The following passage is typical:

A moment later the disk of the sun began to appear, without the slightest vapor obscuring it, and, rising slowly, it seemed an immense wheel of topaz.

.   .   .   .

[The plain] was veiled by a very slight whitish mist and through that transparent gauze we saw . . . its luxuriant groves, its fertile fields, its smiling villages, all of it criss-crossed with roads and paths, along which were already swarming men and cattle. . . . The beautiful gulf of Naples seemed a silver lagoon, and the small lateen boats which crossed it in all directions looked like slight swans. (p. 341)

From the purely literary point of view Rivas' most valuable prose pieces are the three articles which we might classify as *costumbrista*, which appeared in the edition of 1854–55. They are entitled "Los Hércules" (1838), "El hospedador de provincia" ("The Provincial Host"; 1839), and "El ventero" ("The Innkeeper"; 1839).[5] Many writers of the Romantic period wrote *costumbrista* articles, which with more or less realism and frequent irony observed certain national types and customs, occasionally expressing a certain nostalgia at the passing of a particular custom, and often criticizing certain national traits and habits. Though the ironic observation of reality might seem un-Romantic at first, it should be kept in mind that Romanticism does not necessarily eschew realistic description and that the frequent picturesqueness of *costumbrista* descriptions and the occasional nostalgia expressed by the *costumbristas* tie this genre to the Romantic movement.

Of the above-mentioned sketches, "Los Hércules" is the least interesting, though by no means without merit. It is a description of an old promenade in Seville, the Alameda Vieja (Old Public Walk) with its two gigantic pillars known as "los Hércules." There is picturesqueness as well as Romantic nostalgia as the author evokes the promenade's days of glory—when it was filled with *majos* (young men wearing the traditional Andalusian costume), veiled women, horsemen, and friars—and expresses his regret at the passing of the old fiestas with their "cloaks and true mantillas, with capes of silk and the good humor of those times" (p. 334).

"El hospedador de provincia" is an ironic description of a social type which according to the author was going to disappear in a not too distant future. The country gentleman, always ready to place his home at the disposal of a weary traveler was no doubt a blessing in many cases but could apparently also be quite troublesome. In a style reminiscent of a master of *costumbrismo,* Mariano José de Larra,[6] the author speaks of a situation which could come about when a traveler was caught unawares by the hospitality of a typical *hospedador.* The latter might drag him to his house, force him to listen to musical and dramatic recitation by the local talent, and finally, when the traveller is half-starved, feed him a gargantuan meal, whose dishes are for the most part undercooked. The overwhelming character of the *hospedador*'s hospitality is given the dimension of caricature, but this element is mixed with irony and is not without a certain affection for this interesting type, "this plant indigenous to our soil" (p. 319).

"El ventero" is a truly superb piece of writing and makes us wish that Rivas had devoted more time to prose narration. It begins as a *costumbrista* essay describing the typical Spanish inn and typical Spanish innkeeper. In the following passage, the innkeeper is seen through the eyes of a painter, as the author himself indicates. The almost complete absence of verbs in the first half of the paragraph gives us the feeling of a rapidly drawn sketch:

More than forty years old. Dress typical of the area in which the inn is located, but somewhat exaggerated, always with some finery or trimming of the dress of another province. A serious appearance, few words, observing eyes, a mistrustful or superior air, depending on the type of guests who arrive at his house, are characteristics which must be taken into account by any painter who might paint the portrait of an innkeeper. (p. 322)

But after mentioning other characteristics of the innkeeper, the author transforms the sketch into what is essentially a short story, although it has the ring of a true occurrence. It is the story of a "friend" who had to flee in disguise from "one of the most important capitals of Spain" to reach the border with a smuggler as a guide. We suspect strongly that the "friend" is Rivas himself, escaping from Madrid during the revolutionary upheaval of 1836 and making his way to Portugal in disguise with the help of a smuggler. The refugee and his guide, traveling on horseback, arrive at an inn situated in a rather isolated spot. With a few deft strokes, the author describes the gloomy sky at that moment: "The sky seemed of lead, crossed by sinister milk-colored flashes of light, the last efforts of a dying sun" (p. 323). The tall, swarthy inkeeper and his dirty, stupid-looking wife are about to turn the travelers away, when the smuggler utters a few words in a strange dialect and the innkeeper changes his mind "as if by enchantment." There seems to be something mysterious about the inn and its owners, especially as the fugitive notices six or seven shotguns standing in a corner of the kitchen. The interpolated short dialogue as the smuggler asks the woman for food heightens the realism of the scene. After the wife claims there is nothing to eat, a few words from the smuggler, who casts a knowing glance at the shotguns, produce food. The dinner is rapidly eaten and the weary traveler is ushered into a narrow room upstairs where he will spend the night. But he is locked in from outside because, the smuggler explains, there is no way of locking the door from the inside and it would otherwise be knocking on its hinges all night long.

Skillfully, the author lets the mystery deepen, relating how his friend is awakened in the middle of the night by shots, the gallop of horses, voices, the barking of dogs, laughter, and the noise of something like a hoe digging a hole in the corral. In the morning, when the smuggler comes to awaken him, he first denies that anything untoward has happened, then cautions his charge to pretend he has slept soundly and not heard anything, for otherwise his life could be in peril. And he adds ominously: "You do not know what inns and innkeepers are like" (p. 326). In the kitchen downstairs the refugee glimpses bloodstains on the floor and sees that the shotguns are now missing. As the innkeeper hands him a glass of brandy he notices more blood on one of the man's hands and on his shirt. The travelers then leave the inn and after a short ride come upon a rillet of blood which leads to a thicket. The smuggler answers the obvious question of his companion by saying that in the same way that he will not reveal to anyone the name of his charge because the latter has put his faith in him, he will not tell anyone what has happened at the inn, for the innkeeper, too, has faith in him. A few days later, as they separate at the border, the smuggler refuses money proffered by the grateful fugitive but asks his friend to swear that he will never mention the inn nor what he had "dreamed." The traveler makes a solemn promise, and each one goes his way.

Whether true or not, the story is told with consummate skill. We are not told exactly what has happened and can only guess. There is the suggestion that some kind of crime, probably a murder, has taken place, but by whom? And who is the victim? The mystery is complete. The sinister atmosphere is topped by the blood on the floor of the kitchen, on the hand and shirt of the innkeeper, and on the ground outside. The figures of the innkeeper and his wife are soberly, yet vigorously, traced, with a great economy of words. Most interesting is the smuggler. He, too, is a mysterious personage, somewhat sinister and yet with a certain nobility of character. What gives the story its Romantic character is essentially the combination of the smuggler and the unsolved mystery, which from beginning to end hangs over the action. That there can be much realistic observation within a Romantic passage is illustrated here by the crisp description of the activities of the innkeeper and his wife in the kitchen and the occasional but very natural and lively dialogues inserted in the story. The narrative talent which we see in this sketch and Rivas' great narrative and descriptive ability noted throughout his work cause us to agree with Boussagol that, had Rivas been born thirty or forty years later, he would have devoted an important part of his activity to the novel.[7]

CHAPTER 9

Summation

THE Duke of Rivas' literary career can be seen as representative of the trajectory of Spanish literature in the first half of the nineteenth century. Imbued in his youth with the principles of Neoclassicism he began by composing verse in the tradition of such eighteenth-century Neoclassics as Meléndez Valdés and Quintana, also taking as models the great Spanish poets of the sixteenth century such as Garcilaso de la Vega and Fernando de Herrera. His tragedies were constructed with care, but their rather rigid adherence to Neoclassic precepts does little to elicit emotional response in the modern reader. However, even in some early compositions (tragedies as well as narrative poems), we are struck by Saavedra's display of traits that can be called Romantic. We also note that he uses a number of themes from Spanish national history. This is the case of *El paso honroso* (*The Passage at Arms*), of *Florinda,* and of the tragedies *Aliatar, Lanuza,* and *Arias Gonzalo.* The interest and pride of Saavedra in Spain's past was to be an abiding one, and his intense nationalism is characteristic of his art.

Spain and Saavedra were bound sooner or later to break with Neoclassicism since Romanticism began knocking at Spain's door in the 1820's. Although Saavedra would no doubt have abandoned Neoclassic strictures on his own, his exile in England, Malta, and France, and his friendship with John Hookham Frere were factors in his espousal of a new artistic direction. *El moro expósito* (*The Foundling Moor*) signaled the decisive break wtih Neoclassicism, establishing him as an outstanding narrative poet. While it is not the first literary monument of Spanish Romanticism (the first historical novel of López Soler came out in 1830), it is one of those which foreshadowed the path which Romanticism was ultimately to take in Spain.

158

But like Spanish Romanticism as a whole, Rivas had to live through a short period of "revolt," of imitation of the more explosive type of Romanticism, personified in France by Hugo and Dumas. And thus he gave Spain and the world his immortal *Don Alvaro*, with its hero pursued by a relentless fate, its deadly duels, its tragic love and suicide. *Don Alvaro*, though presenting also some very traditional Spanish characteristics, is one of Spain's most "daring" contributions to the repertoire of ultra-Romantic dramas.

Spain, with its tradition of Catholic orthodoxy and nationalism, could not accept the more cosmopolitan type of Romanticism represented by *Don Alvaro* and, a few years later, by the subjectivity and pessimism of Espronceda, and a reaction occurred. Spanish Romanticism turned inward, becoming "nationalized." Spanish Romantics looked more to their own history for inspiration and became satisfied with external characteristics of the movement, i.e., picturesqueness, local color, mixture of the sublime and the trivial, mystery and the macabre.

Rivas' *Romances históricos* (*Historical Ballads*), published in 1841, illustrate perfectly this "nationalization" and present us with what must be considered one of the jewels of this brand of Spanish Romanticism. Rivas is truly at his best here. His talent for presenting sweeping tableaux, for color, for dynamic narrative, and for evoking the macabre reach their highest point in these ballads. He contributes powerfully to the revitalization of the old ballad meter, a process which, begun with Meléndez Valdés in the late eighteenth century, continues until it produces in the twentieth century such masterpieces as García Lorca's *Romancero gitano* (*Collection of Gypsy Ballads*). We find some of the same qualities in Rivas' *Leyendas*, which mark the end of his major poetic achievements, although there is no real artistic advance with respect to the *Romances*. An intense religious faith, accompanied by expressions of nationalism, is one of the dominant aspects of these poems.

Most of the dramas which Rivas wrote in the 1840's were composed with one eye on the Baroque *comedia*. Not outstanding from an artistic point of view, they represent a reaction against cosmopolitan Romanticism. *El desengaño en un sueño* (*Disillusionment in a Dream*) must stand apart, for it represents another effort on the part of Rivas to achieve some philosophical depth in drama. While not as powerful as *Don Alvaro*, it is a stimulating play and stands second only to *Don Alvaro* in Rivas' dramatic achievements. Finally, the later lyrics and the prose sketches are of relatively little value, excepting a few poetic compositions and the exquisite sketch "El ventero," which makes us wonder what heights Rivas would have attained as a novelist.

Notes and References

Chapter One

1. The poet Nicomedes Pastor Díaz (1811–63) wrote the biography of Rivas up to the year 1842. Based at least partly on the material given by the Duke himself, it can be found in Volume I of the *Obras completas* (edition of 1894–1904). The years 1842–65, covered by the Duke's son Enrique R. de Saavedra, are also included in Volume I of this edition.

2. Peers erroneously writes that Victor Hugo spent a short time as a pupil there in 1811 (Edgar Allison Peers, *Angel de Saavedra, Duque de Rivas: A Critical Study* [New York, Paris, 1923], p. 8, n.2). See Gabriel H. Lovett, *Napoleon and the Birth of Modern Spain* (New York, 1965), II, p. 749, n.84.

3. Among his works are the patriotic tragedy *Pelayo* (1805) and poems dealing with freedom of the press, the benefits of smallpox vaccination, Spain's despotic Habsburg monarchy, and Napoleonic aggression against Spain.

4. *Obras completas de Don Angel de Saavedra, Duque de Rivas,* I (Madrid: Sucesores de Rivadeneyra, 1894), 52.

5. Saavedra, Alcalá Galiano, and another official were robbed during their journey to Andalusia. See *Memorias de D. Antonio Alcalá Galiano* (Madrid, 1886), II, p. 415.

6. *Ibid.*, pp. 508–09.

7. Vicente Lloréns, *Liberales y románticos. Una emigración española en Inglaterra (1823–34),* 2d ed. (Madrid: Castalia, 1968), p. 214.

8. *Obras completas,* I, p. 60.

9. *Ibid.*

10. *Ibid.*, pp. 61–62.

11. *Obras completas,* III (1897), vii.

12. See below, pp. 42–44.

13. Edgar Allison Peers, *Rivas: A Critical Study,* p. 55.

14. See Peers, p. 64.

15. See Núñez de Arenas, "El Duque de Rivas, protegido por Mérimée," *Revista de Filología Española,* 15 (1928), 389.

16. *Ibid.*, 390, 396. Margaret A. Williams, "Angel de Saavedra's

Dealings with the French Government, 1830–1833," *Bulletin of Hispanic Studies*, 37 (1960), 112.

17. Núñez de Arenas, 391.

18. It has been thought until recently that, as Saavedra himself indicated, *El moro expósito* was finished in Tours in May, 1833. Margaret A. Williams in a recent article (see above) has shown conclusively that the play must have been finished in Paris, where Saavedra moved from Tours in early March, 1833, and probably during or after June of that year (Margaret A. Williams, 110).

19. "Literature of the Nineteenth Century. Spain," *The Athenaeum*, No. 346 (London, June 14, 1834), p. 452.

20. Quoted in A. K. Shields, "Slidell Mackenzie and the Return of Rivas to Madrid," *Hispanic Review*, 7 (1939), 148. See also Geoffrey Ribbans, "El regreso de Angel de Saavedra de su destierro en 1834," *Revista de Filología Española*, 47 (1964), 421–27. Saavedra's statement about persecution in France must be taken with a grain of salt, though he did have some difficulties in obtaining money from French officialdom.

21. José Zorrilla, *Recuerdos del tiempo viejo* (Barcelona, 1880), I, pp. 138–39.

22. Donald L. Shaw, "Towards the Understanding of Spanish Romanticism," *Modern Language Review*, 58 (1963), 191.

23. Lillian R. Furst, *Romanticism* (London, 1969), p. 27.

24. Donald L. Shaw, 194.

25. René Wellek, "Romanticism Re-examined," *Concepts of Criticism* (New Haven, 1963), p. 220.

26. *Discurso sobre el influjo que ha tenido la crítica moderna en la decadencia del teatro antiguo español y sobre el modo con que debe ser considerado para juzgar convenientemente de su mérito peculiar* (Essay on the Influence which Modern Criticism has had on the Decadence of the Old Spanish Drama and on the Manner in Which it must be considered so that its Characteristic Merit may be Adequately Judged).

27. A Spanish émigré living in England, Telesforo Trueba y Cossío, wrote two novels in English entitled *Gómez Arias* (1828) and *The Castilian* (1829). Practically no first-rate historical novels were written in Spain during the Romantic period. Only with Benito Pérez Galdós (1843–1920) did the Spanish historical novel come of age.

28. For the emergence and development of Romanticism among the Spanish exiles in England, see Lloréns, *Liberales y románticos*.

29. See below, pp. 45–46. On the literary influence of Blanco White on Spanish émigrés, see Lloréns.

30. F. Courtney Tarr, *Romanticism in Spain and Spanish Romanticism: A Critical Survey* (Liverpool, 1939), p. 26.

31. Edgar Allison Peers, *A Short History of the Romantic Movement in Spain* (Liverpool, 1949), p. 71.

32. *Ibid.*

33. There is a great deal of subjectivity and intense and authentic suffering in the poems of Gustavo Adolfo Bécquer (1836–70), but he wrote after the characteristically Romantic period had run its course.

34. See Donald L. Shaw, "The Anti-Romantic Reaction in Spain," *Modern Language Review*, 63 (1968), 606–11.

35. Ángel del Río, "Present Trends in the Conception and Criticism of Spanish Romanticism," *Romanic Review*, 39 (1948), 239.

36. Allison Peers in his monumental *A History of the Romantic Movement in Spain*, 2 vols. (Cambridge, 1940) speaks of a "Romantic Revival" and a "Romantic Revolt." For Peers, Spanish literature is essentially Romantic and is characterized by emphasis on freedom, passion, patriotism, Christianity, and medievalism. Spanish nineteenth-century Romanticism is partly a revival of what had already occurred in other periods, especially the Middle Ages and the seventeenth century, and partly a revolt, due to a certain extent to foreign influences, against Neoclassic restraints. There is some merit in Peers' arguments, but his thesis must be considered somewhat simplistic. While it is true that many Romantics used medieval and Baroque themes and forms, their *Weltanschauung* was not the same as that of medieval man with his far more literal, narrow interpretation of religious doctrine, nor that of the writer of the Baroque period with his totalitarian emphasis on loyalty to Throne and Altar. In the words of Nicholson B. Adams, "artists of the time of the Philips were affected, limited . . . by religious and political postulates no longer valid in the nineteenth century" (Review of Peers' *A History of the Romantic Movement in Spain* in *Hispanic Review*, 9 [1941], 504). The term "Romantic Revival" seems therefore to be of dubious value. More valid is the term "Romantic Revolt," but the author's insistence on classifying some Romantic works under the heading of "Romantic Revival" and others under that of "Romantic Revolt" results in a rather artificial division of works which as a group really represent a new departure in Spanish literature.

37. Nicholson B. Adams, "The Extent of the Duke of Rivas' Romanticism," *Homenaje a Rodríguez-Moñino* (Madrid, 1966), I, 3. Very popular in the 1830's and 1840's was the rather un-Romantic comedy of manners of Bretón de los Herreros (1796–1873).

38. Some critics, including the great Spanish scholar Menéndez

y Pelayo (1856–1912), have seen two distinct trends in Spanish Romanticism represented by two groups of writers: One, conservative and traditionalist in outlook, emphasizing the Christian religion and traditional Spanish values and looking mostly to the Middle Ages and Spain's Golden Age (1500–1680) for inspiration. This would include a majority of Spanish Romantics. Another, cosmopolitan, Byronic in outlook, emphasizing the subjectivity of the poet and disenchantment with the world and society, interested in political liberalism and advocating political and social change. This direction would be represented essentially by Espronceda and Larra and one or two minor poets, and by some of the more daring dramas of the 1830's, including *Don Alvaro*. I have eschewed this approach, for although there was a Byronic, liberal trend in Spanish Romanticism, it is difficult to see two clearly distinguishable groups of writers. For instance, both Espronceda and Larra also wrote a historical novel each, dealing with a medieval theme. Moreover, Espronceda in *El estudiante de Salamanca (The Student of Salamanca)* chose a national, legendary theme and atmosphere, although part of it is Byronic in tone. And Zorrilla, the traditionalist Romantic *par excellence,* wrote some subjective and Byronic poems in his youth. As for *Don Alvaro,* though not really a Byronic drama, it could be considered as containing some indication of disenchantment with the world. Yet Rivas as a whole is definitely on the nationalist side.

39. Quoted by Sergio Fernández de Larraín, "Algo del Duque de Rivas a través de un epistolario en el primer centenario de su muerte," *Atenea* (Santiago de Chile), 411 (1966), 184.

40. *Ibid.,* 227–28.

41. Edgar Allison Peers, *Rivas and Romanticism in Spain* (Liverpool, 1923), p. 2.

Chapter Two

1. *Obras completas,* ed. Jorge Campos, I, *Biblioteca de Autores Españoles,* 100, (Madrid, 1957), p. 21.

2. Quoted by Vicente Lloréns, *Liberales y románticos,* p. 211.

3. "Literature of the Nineteenth Century. Spain," *The Athenaeum,* No. 346 (London, June 14, 1834), p. 452.

4. The first words of the title were *Libro del Passo honroso.* More accessible than this edition is that of 1783, Madrid. See Edgar Allison Peers, *Angel de Saavedra, Duque de Rivas: A Critical Study* (New York, Paris, 1923), p. 137, n.

5. For influences, see Gabriel Boussagol, *Angel de Saavedra, Duc de Rivas. Sa vie, son oeuvre poétique* (Toulouse, Paris, 1926), pp.

153–63. Nicolás Fernández de Moratín (1737–80), father of the famous Neoclassic playwright Leandro Fernández de Moratín, is the author of the epic poem *Las naves de Cortés destruidas* (*The Destruction of the Ships of Cortés*) which influenced Rivas a number of times in his works.

6. Among these we find the great playwright Lope de Vega (1562–1635), who wrote a *Jerusalén conquistada* (*The Conquest of Jerusalem*), a none too successful imitation of Tasso's *Gerusalemme liberata*.

7. The first two cantos are dated London, 1824; the third Gibraltar, 1825; and the last two Malta, 1826.

8. See Ramón Menéndez Pidal, "El rey Rodrigo en la literatura," *Boletín de la Real Academia Española*, 12 (1925), 5–38.

9. Saavedra had to be persuaded to include it along with his *Foundling Moor*. In a foreword he says that if readers gain little from the parts finally published, they lose less from those which were not.

10. See Peers, *Rivas: A Critical Study*, Chapter II, Section 5.

11. *Ibid.*, p. 198.

12. Pastor Díaz and Boussagol indicate that they were not staged. Rivas at the end of Vol. IV of the 1854–55 edition of his collected works indicates that *El Duque de Aquitania* was performed in Seville and other provincial capitals and *Malek-Adhél* in Barcelona.

13. "A Note on Mme. Cottin and the Duke of Rivas," *Hispanic Review*, 15 (1947), 221.

14. *Obras completas*, II, *Biblioteca de Autores Españoles*, 101, p. 121.

15. It was never edited or printed until thirty years after the author's death, in the 1894 edition.

16. It was begun around 1270 under King Alfonso X of Castile and continued around 1289 under King Sancho IV.

17. Manuel Bretón de los Herreros, a prolific playwright, dominated the stage for a long time in the nineteenth century. He began his career as a disciple of Moratín, producing such masterpieces as *A Madrid me vuelvo* (*I am returning to Madrid;* 1828) and *Marcela, o ¿a cuál de los tres?* (*Marcela, Or Which of the Three?;* 1831). After a relatively short excursion into Romanticism he wrote essentially sentimental comedies in which his comic talent shines thanks to his wit and his faithful reproduction of the manners of his time.

Chapter Three

1. See above, p. 19.

2. *Obras completas de D. Angel de Saavedra, Duque de Rivas,* ed. Enrique R. de Saavedra, III (Madrid, 1897), xiii.

3. See Ramón Menéndez Pidal, *La leyenda de los Infantes de Lara* (Madrid, 1896).

4. This meter is called *romance heroico.*

5. "Nicholson B. Adams on *El moro expósito,*" ed. Janet W. Díaz, *Hispanófila,* 52 (1974), 27–28.

6. *Ibid.,* 21.

7. Boussagol, *Angel de Saavedra, Duc de Rivas,* p. 247.

8. A long tabulation of the sources was appended by Peers to his study of Rivas.

9. Boussagol, p. 218.

10. This poem can be consulted in Volume II of the *Biblioteca de Autores Españoles.*

11. Peers, *Rivas: A Critical Study,* p. 361.

12. "Nicholson B. Adams on *El moro expósito,*" 25.

13. Well-known for instance are the *leyendas* in verse of José Zorrilla and the *leyendas* in prose of Gustavo Adolfo Bécquer.

14. *Rivas: A Critical Study,* p. 212.

15. *Ibid.,* p. 211. But Peers also points out that the size of the poem and other factors suggest the epic (*Ibid.,* p. 212).

16. *El Duque de Rivas* in *Escritores españoles e hispanoamericanos* (Madrid, 1884), pp. 46–47.

17. "Poètes modernes de l'Espagne: Le Duc de Rivas," *Revue des Deux Mondes* (1846), I, 338.

18. *La leyenda de los Infantes de Lara,* p. 163.

19. Marcelino Menéndez Pelayo, "*La leyenda de los Infantes de Lara* por Menéndez Pidal," *La Europa Moderna,* 1 (1898), 80 ff., quoted by Angel Crespo, *Aspectos estructurales de El moro expósito del Duque de Rivas* (Uppsala, 1973), p. 81.

20. *El romanticismo en España* (Paris, 1904), p. 54.

21. *Rivas: A Critical Study,* pp. 212–13.

22. Juan Valera, *Obras completas,* 1st ed., II (Madrid, 1942), p. 744.

23. Angel Crespo in his illuminating study of *El moro expósito* points out that because of Mudarra's moral qualities, including his filial piety and his sensitivity, he belongs to the tradition created by Virgil's *Aeneid* rather than to the Homeric epic (*Aspectos estructurales...,* p. 121).

24. *Obras completas,* I, *Biblioteca de Autores Españoles,* 100, p. 259.

25. We do not agree with Boussagol's characterization of Doña Lambra as a vulgar "coquette" (Boussagol, p. 239).

26. While there is comic relief in the heroic epic of Homer and much gaiety in such chivalrous epics as Ariosto's *Orlando Furioso*, there is very little, if any, in the great literary epics (For instance Virgil's *Aeneid*, Camôes' *Os Lusiadas*, Tasso's *Gerusalemme Liberata*, and Milton's *Paradise Lost*). For the question of comic relief in the epic, see C. M. Bowra, *From Virgil to Milton* (London: MacMillan, 1945), pp. 26–28.

27. See the references in the sixth canto to the boring sermon of the archpriest which makes his listeners yawn (p. 173) and in the last canto, to the twenty fat monks "singing hosanna with a hoarse bellowing" (p. 269).

28. The names of Mariano José de Larra and Alcalá Galiano have been mentioned as possible authors of the two articles appearing in the *Revista Española* in May, 1834. We believe that there is a better chance that it was Larra, since Larra was at the time writing for the *Revista Española*.

29. *Revista Española* (May 24, 1834), 505.

30. *Ibid.*, (May 23, 1834), 502.

31. The whole theme of the death of the father of the loved one at the hands of the lover and of the struggle in the soul of the daughter may very well have been inspired by the medieval ballads dealing with the Cid, and by the plays on the same theme by Guillén de Castro and Corneille.

32. See above, p. 54.

33. Constant references are made in the text to God, Heaven, Providence, Destiny, etc.

34. This ending has been criticized by a number of scholars as too abrupt and unexpected. Yet it can be viewed as the working of Divine Providence while also psychologically credible. Kerima may have had a violent conflict in her mind for a long time, being unable to come up with a solution until the very moment of betrothal. She then plausibly decides that she could not marry the slayer of her father.

35. Crespo, p. 126. The role of Providence in *El moro* was mentioned first by Manuele Cañete (Prologue of the 1854–55 edition of Rivas' works, I, xxv), but Crespo has considerably developed the idea.

36. Boussagol, p. 219.

37. *Ibid.*, p. 237.

38. There are some allusions of this kind in *El moro expósito*. See Crespo, p. 70, n.3.

39. "Nicholson B. Adams on *El moro expósito*," p. 26.

40. The exceptions are three songs inserted in the text comprising 128 eight-syllable lines.

41. This work can be read in Volume II of the *Biblioteca de Autores Españoles.*

42. See Crespo, Chapter IX.

Chapter Four

1. Charles of Bourbon, king of Naples from 1734 to 1759, was the son of Philip V of Spain and Elizabeth Farnese. He later ruled as Charles III of Spain from 1759 to 1788.

2. Hurtado and Palencia mention the story of an *indiano* of mysterious origin allegedly told to Rivas in his childhood by a servant of his house (*Historia de la literatura española,* 5th ed., [Madrid, 1943], p. 849).

3. See this theory developed in the article by Walter T. Pattison, "The Secret of Don Alvaro," *Symposium,* 21 (1967), 67–81.

4. See Leopoldo Augusto de Cueto, *Discurso necrológico literario en elogio del Excmo. Sr. Duque de Rivas* (Madrid, 1866), p. 89, n.1.

5. Quoted by Peers, *Rivas: A Critical Study,* p. 446. See this work, pp. 444–448, for Byronic parallels with *Don Alvaro.*

6. Boussagol, *Angel de Saavedra, Duc de Rivas,* p. 267.

7. *Ibid.,* p. 264. Jovellanos' *El delincuente honrado* may be read in Volume 46 of the *Biblioteca de Autores Españoles.* The play itself is discussed by John H. R. Polt in *Gaspar Melchor de Jovellanos* (New York: Twayne, 1971).

8. See Peers, *Rivas: A Critical Study,* pp. 458–63.

9. Cueto, p. 87. Mérimée, in a letter to Cueto, claimed that he had found the story of the monk's duel with the brother of the seduced woman in some old "mémoires" (*Ibid.,* p. 88, n.).

10. The original version of *Don Alvaro* is not extant.

11. Boussagol, p. 279.

12. Juan Valera, *Obras completas,* II, p. 747. Another Spaniard went so far as to claim that Mérimée actually translated *Don Alvaro* into French (See Enrique Funes, *Don Alvaro o la fuerza del sino. Estudio crítico* [Madrid, 1899], pp. 63–64, n.1).

13. See Boussagol, pp. 280–81.

14. There is an outside chance that, rather than deriving his material directly from Rivas, Mérimée consulted some sources also used by the Spaniard. As Francisco Caravaca points out, some of this material may have been suggested to the French author by Spanish friends such as Countess Montijo (see Francisco Caravaca, "¿Plagió Mérimée el 'Don Alvaro' del Duque de Rivas?," *La Torre,* Año 13 [1965], 116).

15. See the prologue of Pilar Díez y Jiménez-Castellanos to *Don Alvaro* (Zaragoza, 1966), pp. 19–20.
16. Donald L. Shaw, *A Literary History of Spain. The Nineteenth Century* (London, New York, 1972), p. 11.
17. *Obras completas*, II, *Biblioteca de Autores Españoles*, 101, p. 306.
18. Peers, p. 398.
19. In the last act Alfonso reveals to Don Alvaro that his parents have been pardoned by the King of Spain.
20. "The Secret of Don Alvaro," *Symposium*, 21 (1967), 78.
21. Don Alvaro is more complex than either Doña Leonor or her brothers, but he reacts quite predictably to love and to insult.
22. *"Don Alvaro* or the Force of Cosmic Injustice," *Studies in Romanticism*, 12 (1973), 560. However, Cardwell's interpretation of the racial theme in a strictly symbolic way as standing for "nonconformity, unorthodoxy, a challenge to the traditional view of the universe and its structure" (*Ibid.*, 566) seems far-fetched.
23. See his reference to the sun as the protector of his sovereign lineage, Act I, scene 7.
24. Notwithstanding these allusions to the devil, we think that E. Grey makes too much of them when he interprets Don Alvaro as a metaphor of Satan (see "Satanism in *Don Alvaro*," *Romanische Forschungen*, 80 [1968], 292–302).
25. Paul Van Tieghem, *Le romantisme dans la littérature européenne* (Paris, 1948), p. 264.
26. José de Espronceda, *Obras poéticas*, ed. Moreno Villa (Madrid: Espasa Calpe, 1962), I, 240–41.
27. "C'est elle qui marque le point de vue du drame" ("It is this [unity] which provides the point of view of the play," Victor Hugo, *La Préface du 'Cromwell*,' ed. Edmond Wahl [Oxford: The Clarendon Press, 1909], p. 30). For Victor Hugo's discussion of the three unities see this edition, pp. 27–30.
28. *La Préface du 'Cromwell*,' p. 11. Victor Hugo in the *Préface* and other French Romantics like Alfred de Vigny emphasize the difference between Neoclassic tragedy and Romantic drama. They point out that Romantic drama rejects the unities of time and place and keeps only the unity of action, and even that can be replaced by the unity of interest. Romantic drama demands the mixture of the sublime and the grotesque. While Neoclassic theater takes its subject matter from Greek or Roman history, Romantic theater seeks them in modern history. Romantic theater eliminates a number of Neoclassic conventions such as confidants and dreams. Unlike Neoclassic theater, Romantic theater looks for the picturesque and for

violence on the stage. While Neoclassic theater presents characters who reason and engage in self-analysis, Romantic theater is dominated by blind impulses, mystery, and fate.

29. The term *costumbrismo* means the portraying of everyday life and prevailing customs. During the Romantic period many Romantic writers wrote realistic sketches portraying typical scenes of contemporary life and often emphasizing the characteristic and the picturesque. The three most important *costumbristas* were Mariano José de Larra (1809–37), Ramón de Mesonero Romanos (1803–82), and Serafín Estébanez Calderón (1799–1867).

30. José Martínez Ruiz (Azorín), *Rivas y Larra; razón social del romanticismo en España* (Madrid, 1916), p. 59.

31. Joaquín Casalduero, "*Don Alvaro* o el destino como fuerza," in *Estudios sobre el teatro español* (Madrid, 1962), p. 247. The first *décima* of Segismundo's famous soliloquy reads as follows: "I intend to find out, Heavens, / Since you treat me in this fashion, / What crime I have committed / Against you by being born, / Although if I was born, I understand / What crime I have committed: / Your justice and rigor / Has had enough cause, / Since the greatest crime / Of Man is to have been born."

32. *Rivas y Larra,* p. 28.

33. *Ibid.,* p. 33.

34. Peers, p. 430.

35. Cardwell, "*Don Alvaro* or the Force of Cosmic Injustice," 570.

36. Pastor Díaz, *Vida del autor* in *Obras completas* I (1894), p. 70.

37. *Galería de la literatura española* (Madrid, 1846), p. 106.

38. *Revue des Deux Mondes* (1846), I, 347.

39. Francisco Blanco García, *La literatura española en el siglo XIX,* 3rd. ed., I (Madrid, 1909), p. 149, n.1.

40. "La historia externa e interna de España en la primera mitad del siglo XIX," *Estudios y discursos de crítica histórica y literaria,* VII, in *Obras completas,* XII (Santander, 1942), p. 269.

41. Ernest Mérimée, *Précis d'Histoire de la littérature espagnole,* 2nd. ed. (Paris, n.d.), p. 425.

42. *Discurso necrológico,* pp. 92–93.

43. *El Duque de Rivas* in *Escritores españoles e hispanoamericanos,* p. 58.

44. Enrique Funes, *Don Alvaro o la fuerza del sino. Estudio crítico* (Madrid, 1899), pp. 96–97.

45. *La literatura española en el siglo XIX,* I, p. 148 n.

46. Peers, p. 392.

47. *Ibid.,* p. 405.

48. Richard Cardwell, 560.

49. *Ibid.,* 561.
50. *Ibid.,* 574.
51. See Margaret A. Williams, "Angel de Saavedra's Dealings with the French Government, 1830–1833," *Bulletin of Hispanic Studies,* 37 (1960), 106–14.
52. For instance: "Within a few hours, / Far from vain and deceitful worldly affections, / I shall go to the severe tribunal of God!" (p. 349).

Chapter Five

1. *La muerte de un caballero* (*The Death of a Knight*).
2. The Spanish *verso de romance* or ballad meter consists of seven-, eight-, or nine-syllable lines, all counting theoretically as eight-syllable verses. The seventh syllable is always stressed. In assonance, only vowels correspond. If the even-numbered lines have seven syllables (*verso agudo*), the last stressed vowel is the same. If they have eight (*verso llano*), a combination of the same two vowels at the end of the verse, the first being stressed, is found throughout the even lines. Nine-syllable *verso de romance* lines are rare.
3. Although Rivas had written ballads in his youth, most of these were lyrical compositions, written in the Neoclassic style in imitation of the eighteenth-century poet Juan Meléndez Valdés and singing of love and often of shepherds and shepherdesses. They were a far cry from the old *romances,* in which the epic, narrative element played a large role.
4. See Menéndez Pidal, *Romancero hispánico. Teoría e historia,* 2 vols. (Madrid: Espasa Calpe, 1953).
5. The old romances were probably first written in sixteen-syllable lines, divided into two hemistiches separated by a caesura, and with assonance at the end of each line.
6. The Neoclassic poet Juan Meléndez Valdés made a brave effort in the latter half of the eighteenth century and the early 1800's to revive the *romance,* which had fallen on evil times. In particular he wrote an unfinished poem composed of two *romances,* entitled *Doña Elvira,* which can be considered a forerunner of the *Romances históricos* and of the *leyendas* of Zorrilla.
7. The German scholars Jacob Grimm and Depping published anthologies of Spanish *romances* in 1815 and 1817 respectively, and Lockhardt brought out his English translation of many Spanish ballads in 1823.
8. Some of the more important nineteenth- and twentieth-century collections of *romances* are Durán's *Romancero general,* published

between 1828 and 1849, and later republished in Volumes 10 and 16 of the *Biblioteca de Autores Españoles;* Wolf's *Primavera y flor de romances* (Berlin, 1856); Menéndez Pidal's *Flor nueva de romances viejos* (Madrid, 1933); and Santullano's *Romancero español,* 5th ed. (Madrid: Aguilar, 1946).

9. Rivas is alluding here to the eleven- and seven-syllable lines taken from Italian poetry in the sixteenth century.

10. *Obras completas,* III, *Biblioteca de Autores Españoles,* 102, p. 401.

11. Rivas cannot be faulted too much for his views on the origin of the *romances,* since they were also held by a number of scholars in the nineteenth century.

12. Enrique Gil y Carrasco, "*Romances históricos* por Don Angel Saavedra, Duque de Rivas," *Obras completas, Biblioteca de Autores Españoles,* 74 (Madrid: Atlas, 1954), p. 515.

13. See Boussagol, pp. 283–85.

14. *Obras completas,* I, *Biblioteca de Autores Españoles,* 100, 339.

15. According to Boussagol the historical source for this *romance* are Chapters 137 and 139 of the *Crónica de los Reyes Católicos* by "El Cura de los Palacios" (Boussagol, p. 301).

16. Italics ours.

17. Boussagol gives as a source of this *romance* as well as of *La victoria de Pavía* Prudencio de Sandoval's *Historia de la vida y hechos del Emperador Carlos V* (1604–06; Boussagol, pp. 299–300).

18. Cf. *Duque de Rivas. Romances,* ed. Rivas Cherif, I (Madrid: Espasa Calpe, 1966), pp. 272–73, n.

19. According to Boussagol, Rivas had read in Sandoval that the Count of Benavente had refused the Order of the Golden Fleece because it was of foreign origin, and the poet had thus received the inspiration for his story (Boussagol, p. 301).

20. See my "Napoleon in 19th Century Spanish Letters," *Romance Notes,* 13 (1971).

21. The lyric quality of a number of stanzas in *Bailén,* including the six in the third part using a different and shorter meter, has led some critics to write that the poem often strikes a lyric note that brings it closer to the patriotic ode than to the true *romance* (see Boussagol, pp. 294–95).

22. This intervention of the Almighty may indicate the influence of Fernando de Herrera's famous sixteenth-century ode to the victory of Lepanto (1571) over the Turks, in which God gives the upper hand to His chosen people, the Spaniards.

23. This *romance* was published in March, 1838 in the *Liceo Artístico y Literario Español.* Boussagol gives as the main source the

Anales eclesiásticos y seculares de la ciudad de Sevilla (1677) by Diego Ortiz de Zúñiga (Boussagol, p. 287).

24. See below, pp. 113–14.

25. Boussagol indicates that this *romance* was partly inspired by the *Crónica del rey Don Pedro* by Pero López de Ayala (1332–1407), (Boussagol, pp. 250, 259).

26. Boussagol gives as sources the *Crónica del rey Don Pedro* by Pero López de Ayala and the *Romance of the History of Spain* (1827) by the Spanish emigré Telesforo de Trueba y Cossío (1799–1835), written in England and containing legends based on the Spanish *romancero* (Boussagol, pp. 289–92). Rivas probably drew his inspiration not from the English version but from the French translation *L'Espagne romantique* (1832).

27. Boussagol, p. 291.

28. Boussagol's explanation that Rivas wrote three ballads on this subject because Don Pedro reminded him of his beloved Seville, because Rivas did not consider it beneath him to repeat the same themes, and perhaps because Trueba in his preface to *The Castilian*, published in England in 1829, had noted that the age of Don Pedro offers striking and Romantic incidents (Boussagol, p. 289), seems insufficient.

29. Boussagol indicates as the main source the *Centón epistolario del bachiller Fernán Gómez de Cibdarreal* (Boussagol, pp. 253–57).

30. Boussagol gives as the source the *Vida del grande San Francisco de Borja* by Cardinal Alvaro de Cienfuegos (Boussagol, p. 293).

31. The historical novel, especially that of Walter Scott, is a good example of how Romantic and realistic elements mesh. Another example is the presence of *costumbrista* scenes in *Don Alvaro*.

32. The author here uses terms dear to the Neoclassics.

33. Together with Trueba's *The Romance of the History of Spain* the inspiration for this *romance* was perhaps the play *Antonio Pérez y Felipe II* by J. Muñoz Maldonado, performed in Madrid in October, 1837 (Boussagol, p. 297).

34. The Neoclassic poet Manuel José Quintana, Rivas' model for many of his early poems, also takes a negative view of Philip II in his poem *El panteón del Escorial* (1805), but the ghost of his Philip II speaks of his reign with a certain grandeur which mitigates somewhat the horrible impression made at first.

35. Historians today incline more to the theory that Antonio Pérez was the prime mover of the murder of Escobedo and convinced the King to authorize this foul act.

36. See for instance the historical drama *El haz de leña* (*The Bundle of Firewood*) by Gaspar Núñez de Arce (1872).

37. One of the military-religious orders founded in Castile in the Middle Ages.

38. Moslems born on the Iberian Peninsula and nominally converted to Christianity in 1502.

39. The Order of the Golden Fleece was established in Burgundy in 1429.

40. Italics ours.

41. Peers, *Rivas: A Critical Study*, p. 495.

42. *Rivas y Larra*, p. 17.

43. In this connection see Boussagol, pp. 396–98.

44. Cipriano de Rivas Cherif, *Duque de Rivas. Romances* (Madrid: La Lectura, 1911), I, 19.

Chapter Six

1. *La azucena milagrosa* was dedicated to Rivas' young friend, the Romantic poet José Zorrilla, who himself had dedicated his own *La azucena silvestre* (*The Wild Lily*), written shortly before, to Rivas. *La azucena milagrosa* was first published in 1851 as part of a collection of Rivas' verses.

2. Prologue to *Obras completas*, III (Madrid, 1854), p. 335.

3. Cañete, *El Duque de Rivas*, p. 93.

4. The *romance heroico* consists of hendecasyllables, whose even-numbered lines are in assonance.

5. The supernatural also plays an important role in the *leyendas* of José Zorrilla, who composed many poems belonging to this genre.

6. *Obras completas*, I, *Biblioteca de Autores Españoles*, 100, p. 430.

7. The Visigothic king who became a Catholic in 589 A.D. and officially established Catholicism in Spain.

8. See the figure of Elvira in *El estudiante de Salamanca* by Espronceda. Some of the lines describing her are as follows:

A woman! Is it perhaps
A white solitary nymph,
Who in the moonlight
Wanders mysteriously?

Her dress is white, her hair
Undulates looosely on her shoulder. (José de Espronceda, *Obras poéticas*, I, ed. Moreno Villa, [Madrid: Espasa Calpe, 1962], 196.)

9. The *quintilla* has generally five rhyme schemes: *ababa; abaab;*

abbab; aabab, and *aabba.* Not more than two consonant rhymes may follow each other.
10. The *redondilla* is a four-verse stanza used for lively dialogue.
11. See J. P. Wickersham Crawford, "The Braggart Soldier and the *Rufián* in the Spanish Drama of the Sixteenth Century," *Romanic Review,* 2 (1911), 186–208.
12. See above. p. 111.

Chapter Seven

1. Some of the characteristics of the Baroque or Golden Age *comedia* are: The preponderance of action over ideological depth; the non-observance of the unities of time and place and the somewhat loose observance of the unity of action; complication of the action, with the frequent presence of a secondary plot; the presence of both comic and tragic elements; the prominence of the themes of love, honor, and loyalty to Throne and Altar; numerous characters; the presence of a *gracioso* or comic servant, who is often a repository of popular wisdom; a variety of meters; and highly metaphoric language. For a useful introduction, see Margaret Wilson, *Spanish Drama of the Golden Age* (Oxford, New York: Pergamon Press, 1969).
2. *Rivas: A Critical Study,* pp. 529, n.1; 530.
3. *Obras completas,* II, *Biblioteca de Autores Españoles,* 101, p. 365, n.1.
4. *Ibid.,* III, *Biblioteca de Autores Españoles,* 102, p. 365.
5. *Comedia de capa y espada.* The term *comedia* was used in the sevententh century to designate true comedies as well as tragicomedies and tragedies.
6. *Obras completas,* II, *Biblioteca de Autores Españoles,* 101, p. 422.
7. *Obras completas,* III, *Biblioteca de Autores Españoles,* 102, p. 13.
8. Actually there are two *graciosos,* the feminine counterpart of Berrio being Sancha; but Berrio has a more important role.
9. *El Duque de Rivas, Escritores españoles e hispanoamericanos,* p. 71.
10. *Discurso necrológico,* p. 94.
11. *Rivas: A Critical Study,* p. 538.
12. *Ibid.,* p. 545.
13. The author and date of the original play are not known. "The *comedia de magia* . . . was in essence a play in which apparatus is used on the stage to produce effects ridiculously marvellous: tree-

trunks walk, palaces fly, furniture assumes life; human beings vanish, take inanimate form or appear from nowhere. The characters are entirely divorced from reality; the plot is a mere string of impossible happenings" (E. Allison Peers, *A History of the Romantic Movemen in Spain* [Cambridge, 1940], I, p. 34).

14. It has been suggested that Rivas, while wishing to write a philosophical play, was aware of the success the *comedias de magia* were enjoying on Spanish stages and hence wrote a drama in this manner (see Richard B. O'Connell, "Rivas' *El desengaño en un sueño* and Grillparzer's *Der Traum ein Leben*: A Problem in Assessment of Influence," *Philosophical Quarterly*, 40 [1961], 575. See also the unpublished Ph.D. thesis by Douglas Richard Hilt, "A. W. Schlegel and His Theories of Romanticism as Reflected in Parallel Plays of Grillparzer and Rivas," University of Arizona, 1967, pp. 98, 141).

15. See *Rivas: A Critical Study*, pp. 547–49.

16. See Peers, pp. 550–51.

17. See Peers, pp. 552–57.

18. O'Connell, 573.

19. *Ibid.*, 575.

20. For a full discussion see O'Connell's article.

21. "An Archetypal Analysis of Rivas' *El desengaño en un sueño*," *Bulletin of Hispanic Studies*, 45 (1968), 201.

22. *Ibid.*

23. *Ibid.*, 208.

24. A famous example is the poem by the sixteenth-century ascetic Fray Luis de León, entitled *Vida retirada* (*Secluded Life*), in which he praises the quiet country life.

25. Allen, 211.

26. *Ibid.*

Chapter Eight

1. See for instance the passage about the love of Elvira for Don Félix in *El estudiante de Salamanca* by Espronceda and the same author's "Canto a Teresa" in his *El diablo mundo*. These passages can be read in the *Clásicos Castellanos* (Espasa Calpe) edition of Espronceda's works.

2. *Obras completas*, I, *Biblioteca de Autores Españoles*, 100, p. 516.

3. It was first published in Madrid in 1848.

4. *Obras completas*, III, *Biblioteca de Autores Españoles*, 102, p. 150.

5. "Los Hércules" first appeared in Seville in the periodical *La Lira Andaluza* in 1838. "El hospedador de provincia" and "El ventero" were published first in the *costumbrista* collection *Los españoles pintados por sí mismos* (*Spaniards Painted by Themselves;* Madrid, 1843–44).

6. We are particularly reminded of one of Larra's most famous articles, "El castellano viejo" ("The Old Castilian"), in which an old-fashioned Spanish patriot forces a reluctant friend to attend a most bothersome dinner party. Rivas was no doubt heavily influenced by Larra when he wrote this article.

7. Boussagol, p. 341.

Selected Bibliography

PRIMARY SOURCES

Poesías de Don Angel de Saavedra Remírez de Baquedano (Cadiz: Imprenta Patriótica, 1814). The first collection of Saavedra's works; contains *El paso honroso.*

Poesías de Don Angel de Saavedra Remírez de Baquedano. 2 volumes (Madrid: Imprenta de Sancha, 1820–21). Seven compositions not included in the first edition appear here. The second volume contains *El paso honroso,* with changes, and two tragedies: *El Duque de Aquitania* and *Malek-Adhél.*

El moro expósito, o Córdoba y Burgos en el siglo décimo. 2 volumes (Paris: Librería Hispano-Americana, 1834). *El moro expósito* begins in the first volume and ends in the second, which also contains *Florinda,* five historical *romances,* and some short poems, including "El faro de Malta." Dedication to John Hookham Frere, with the unsigned prologue to *El moro expósito* by Alcalá Galiano.

Don Alvaro o la fuerza del sino (Madrid: Imprenta de Tomás Jordán, 1835). Dedication to Alcalá Galiano.

Romances históricos (Paris: Librería de D. Vicente Salvá, 1841). Eighteen *romances,* preceded by the author's prologue. First edition of all the collected historical ballads, followed in the same year by that of Lalama, Madrid.

Obras completas. 5 volumes (Madrid: Imprenta de la Biblioteca Nueva, 1854–55). Not truly complete (the early tragedies and *El parador de Bailén* are missing). Important prologues by Cañete and Ochoa; biography of Rivas by Pastor Díaz. Vol. II contains *El moro expósito,* with dedication to Frere and prologue by Alcalá Galiano, this time naming the author.

Obras completas. 2 volumes (Barcelona: Montaner y Simón, 1884–85). Not complete (lacks early tragedies and *El parador de Bailén*). Alcalá Galiano's prologue to *El moro expósito* is omitted.

Obras completas. 7 volumes (Madrid: Sucesores de Rivadeneyra, 1894–1904). Not complete (of the tragedies only *Arias Gonzalo* and *Lanuza* are given). *El desengaño en un sueño* and *El parador de Bailén* are omitted, as are all the prose works. Con-

tains both the dedication to Frere and Alcalá Galiano's pro-
logue to *El moro expósito*, and biographies of Rivas by Pastor
Díaz (up to 1842) and Enrique de Saavedra (1842–65).
Romances históricos. 2 volumes, ed. Cipriano Rivas Cherif, *Clásicos
Castellanos* (Madrid: La Lectura, 1911–12). Introduction and
notes, appendices, including Alcalá Galiano's prologue to *El
moro expósito.*
Don Alvaro o la fuerza del sino, ed. Lewis E. Brett, in *Nineteenth
Century Spanish Plays* (New York: Appleton-Century-Crofts,
1935). Thoroughly annotated.
Obras completas (Madrid: Aguilar, 1945). Not complete as some
early poems are missing, as well as Alcalá Galiano's prologue to *El
moro expósito.* Introduction by Enrique Ruiz de la Serna.
Obras completas. 3 volumes, ed. Jorge Campos, in the *Biblioteca de
Autores Españoles,* vols. 100–102 (Madrid: Ediciones Atlas,
1957). The most complete of Rivas' collected works; however,
does not include Alcalá Galiano's prologue nor the biographies
by Pastor Díaz and Enrique de Saavedra.
Don Alvaro o la fuerza del sino, ed. Alberto Sánchez (Salamanca:
Anaya, 1959).
Don Alvaro o la fuerza del sino, ed. by Pilar Díez y Jiménez-Cas-
tellanos, *Biblioteca Clásica Ebro* (Zaragoza: Ebro, 1966).
Thoroughly annotated, with an extensive introduction.
El moro expósito (Madrid: Taurus, 1967). Introduction by Elias
Torre Pintueles with biographical data.

SECONDARY SOURCES

ADAMS, NICHOLSON B. "The Extent of the Duke of Rivas' Romanticism," *Homenaje a Rodríguez-Moñino* (Madrid: Castalia, 1966),
I, 1–7. This important article makes the point that Rivas' gradual
adoption of certain Romantic principles culminated with *Don
Alvaro* in 1835 and did not increase thereafter.
——. "Nicholson B. Adams on *El moro expósito,*" edited by
Janet W. Díaz, *Hispanófila,* 52 (1974), 11–33. Provides a useful summary of the work and a most thorough study of the
sources.
ALLEN, RUPERT C. "An Archetypal Analysis of Rivas' *El desengaño
en un sueño,*" *Bulletin of Hispanic Studies,* 45 (1968), 201–15.
Argues that *El desengaño en un sueño* is a mythic play dramatizing the psychological transformation of a young man and
that the primary motivation of the story is supplied by a
struggle of wills between father and son.

BORDATO, ELISA ESTHER. "Mérimée y el duque de Rivas," *Humanidades* (La Plata, Argentina), 21 (1930), 233–46. Analyzes the similarities between Mérimée's *Les âmes du purgatoire* and Rivas' *Don Alvaro* pointing out differences. Does not arrive at any significant conclusion with regard to the mystery of the resemblance of the two works.

BOUSSAGOL, GABRIEL. "Angel de Saavedra, Duc de Rivas. Essai de bibliographie critique," *Bulletin Hispanique*, 29 (1927), 5–98. An indispensable bibliographical guide.

––––––. *Angel de Saavedra, Duc de Rivas. Sa vie, son oeuvre poétique* (Toulouse: Privat, 1926). A most thorough study of Rivas' life and works. A great deal of emphasis is placed on biographical data, influences, and sources, but a large section of the book is devoted to Rivas' skill as a writer. The author uses a topical approach as against an analysis in depth, a procedure which occasionally leaves the impression that he has not completely come to grips with the works themselves.

CAÑETE, MANUEL. *El Duque de Rivas* in *Escritores españoles e hispanoamericanos* (Madrid: Tello, 1884). A valuable though rather short study of Rivas' life and works. Insists on a Providentialist interpretation of *El moro expósito* and *Don Alvaro*.

CARAVACA, FRANCISCO. "¿Plagió Mérimée el 'Don Alvaro' del Duque de Rivas?" *La Torre*, Año 13 (1965), 77–135. Seems convinced that Mérimée got his inspiration for *Les âmes du purgatoire* from Rivas' *Don Alvaro* but adduces no conclusive proof.

CARDWELL, RICHARD A. "*Don Alvaro* or the Force of Cosmic Injustice," *Studies in Romanticism*, 12 (1973), 559–79. Argues that *Don Alvaro* is a symbolic play in which the hero voices the misgivings of an influential minority of the age concerning traditional interpretations of the universe and man's status and role within it.

CASALDUERO, JOAQUÍN. "*Don Alvaro* o el destino como fuerza," in *Estudios sobre el teatro español* (Madrid: Gredos, 1962). Contains interesting comments on the uniqueness of Romantic art as opposed to Neoclassicism and Baroque.

CASTRO, AMÉRICO. *Les grands romantiques espagnols* (Paris: La Renaissance du Livre, 1923). Short anthology of some of Spanish Romanticism's masterpieces, preceded by an introduction which could still stand as a model of the genre. Among its merits is a lucid differentiation between the Romantic spirit and the spirit of Calderón's theater.

CRESPO, ÁNGEL. *Aspectos estructurales de El moro expósito del Duque de Rivas* (Uppsala: Almqvist and Wiksell, 1973). A detailed and illuminating analysis of *El moro expósito*, it devotes considerable space to the role of Providence in the structure of the poem.

CUETO, LEOPOLDO AUGUSTO. DE. *Discurso necrológico literario en elogio del Excmo. Sr. Duque de Rivas* (Madrid: Rivadeneyra, 1866). Provides interesting glimpses of Rivas' character and keen insights into his work, particularly *Don Alvaro* and *El desengaño en un sueño.*

DEL RÍO, ÁNGEL. "Present Trends in the Conception and Criticism of Spanish Romanticism," *Romanic Review*, 39 (1948), 229–48. Still one of the most important articles on Spanish Romanticism in this century; maintains that Spanish Romanticism, foreign in its origin, became more and more nationalized because it was impossible for the unorthodox and revolutionary philosophy of the European movement to take root in the Catholic soil of Spain.

DÍAZ-PLAJA, GUILLERMO. *Introducción al estudio del romanticismo español*, 2nd edition (Madrid: Espasa Calpe, 1942). Examines the concept of Romanticism from the point of view of Spanish texts written by contemporaries; divides Spanish Romanticism into a traditionalist branch and a "liberal" branch. Penetrating remarks on the main themes of Romanticism.

FERRER, DEL RÍO, ANTONIO. *Galería de la literatura española* (Madrid: Mellado, 1846). The chapter on Rivas is of little value as far as analysis of works is concerned.

FUNES, ENRIQUE. *Don Alvaro o la fuerza del sino. Estudio crítico* (Madrid: Victoriano Suárez, 1899). Concentrates on the traditionalist aspects of *Don Alvaro* and what the author considers is its highly orthodox Catholic meaning.

FURST, LILLIAN R. *Romanticism* (London: Methuen, 1969). Useful introduction to European Romanticism.

GARCÍA MERCADAL, J. *Historia del romanticismo en España* (Barcelona: Labor, 1943). Useful survey of the important Romantic authors and their works, preceded by an informative introduction dealing with European Romanticism. For García Mercadal, Spanish literary Romanticism was preceded by a political Romanticism beginning with the anti-Napoleonic uprising of 1808 and continuing with the liberal experiments of 1812 and 1820–23.

GONZÁLEZ RUIZ, NICOLÁS. *El Duque de Rivas o la fuerza del sino*, 2nd edition (Madrid: Aspas, 1944). Biography of the poet; concerned more with the political background of his activities than with his literary creations. The "power of fate" of the

Selected Bibliography 183

title refers to the historical events through which the Duke lived and against which he was at times forced to struggle.

KING, EDMUND L. "What Is Spanish Romanticism?," *Studies in Romanticism*, 2 (1962), 1–11. Highly stimulating article which makes too much, however, of the theory that Spanish Romanticism was nothing more than pseudo-Romanticism.

LIÑÁN Y EGUIZÁBAL, JOSÉ DE. "El Duque poeta," *Revista de Historia y de Genealogía Española*, Segunda Época, 4 (1930), 321–47; 401–56. Standard biography based on Pastor Díaz and Enrique de Saavedra, but with some additional material discovered by the author.

LLORÉNS CASTILLO, VICENTE. *Liberales y románticos. Una emigración española en Inglaterra (1823–1834)*, 2nd edition (Madrid: Castalia, 1968). Important study of the literary activities in England of the Spanish emigrés of 1823–34; among other things shows how Romanticism took hold in these circles before it really got under way in Spain.

MARTÍNEZ RUIZ, JOSÉ. *Rivas y Larra; razón social del romanticismo en España* (Madrid: Renacimiento, 1916). Study of two of the most important figures of Spanish Romanticism; contains a detailed analysis of *Don Alvaro*, with many unjustified criticisms.

NAVAS RUIZ, RICARDO. *El romanticismo español. Historia y crítica* (Madrid, Salamanca: Anaya, 1970). Thorough, valuable study of the Romantic movement in Spain. The subject is treated through an over-all analysis of Spanish Romanticism and through a study of the most important Romantic authors.

O'CONNELL, RICHARD B. "'Rivas' *El desengaño en un sueño* and Grillparzer's *Der Traum ein Leben*: A Problem in Assessment of Influence," *Philological Quarterly*, 40 (1961), 569–76. Discussion of the similarity between these two plays. O'Connell concludes that Grillparzer and Rivas probably utilized the same source.

PASTOR DÍAZ, NICOMEDES. "Biography of Rivas" in Volume II of *Galería de españoles célebres contemporáneos* (Madrid, 1843), directed by Pastor Díaz and Francisco de Cárdenas. Reprinted in the 1854 and 1894 editions. Pastor Díaz was a friend of Rivas and the biography was partly written from material supplied by the Duke himself. Occasionally, however, it is incorrect.

PATTISON, WALTER T. "The Secret of Don Alvaro," *Symposium*, 21 (1967), 67–81. Argues that Don Alvaro's unwillingness to tell about his mixed blood is the key to his psychology, his fate, and the structure of the play.

PEERS, EDGAR ALLISON. *A History of the Romantic Movement in Spain,* 2 volumes (Cambridge: The University Press, 1940). Studies the Romantic movement in the greatest detail. The thesis of Peers, which in recent years has come under increasing criticism, is that Spanish literature is essentially "Romantic" and that the Romantic movement in Spain, which blossomed only for a short time, to be replaced by Eclecticism, was composed of a revival of the Romantic aspects of Spanish literature plus a revolt against neoclassic strictures.

—————. *A Short History of the Romantic Movement in Spain* (Liverpool: Institute of Hispanic Studies, 1949). Useful abridgement of the two-volume *A History of the Romantic Movement in Spain.*

—————. *Angel de Saavedra, Duque de Rivas: A Critical Study* (published as vol. 58 of the *Revue Hispanique,* Paris, New York, 1923). A most thorough study of the work of Rivas, characterized by painstaking scholarship. The English critic gives a complete biography and studies each of the important works of Rivas in turn. Some of his views, however, seem dated today. Includes a valuable bibliography.

—————. *Rivas and Romanticism in Spain* (Liverpool: The University Press of Liverpool, 1923). Advancing some ideas developed later in *A History of the Romantic Movement in Spain,* Peers sees in Rivas both the signs of Romantic "revival" (*El moro expósito*) and "revolt" (*Don Alvaro*) and indicates that Rivas' Romanticism was a growth and not the result of a conversion. In a second part devoted to Rivas' art, the critic examines the use the poet made of light and color, the theme of Andalusia in his poems, the importance of religion in his work, and the influence of England.

PIÑEYRO, ENRIQUE. *El romanticismo en España* (Paris: Garnier, 1904). Competent discussion of the main figures of the Spanish Romantic period, but one misses an over-all treatment of Spanish Romanticism, which the title seems to promise.

SHAW, DONALD L. *A Literary History of Spain. The Nineteenth Century* (London, New York: Benn, Barnes and Noble, 1972). Contains three excellent chapters on Spanish Romanticism.

—————. "Towards the Understanding of Spanish Romanticism," *Modern Language Review,* 58 (1963), 190–95. Argues that the origins of Spanish Romanticism must be sought in the European metaphysical crisis of the end of the eighteenth century.

TARR, F. COURTNEY. *Romanticism in Spain and Spanish Romanticism: A Critical Survey* (Liverpool: Institute of Hispanic Studies,

1939). One of the theses of Tarr's perceptive essay is that in the theater, Spanish Romanticism on the French model ended about 1837 and that a peculiarly Spanish brand of Romantic drama developed after that date.

VALERA, JUAN. *Don Angel de Saavedra, Duque de Rivas* in *Obras completas,* II (Madrid: Aguilar, 1942), 716–53. Argues that *El paso honroso* is Romantic and that Frere did not have to convert Saavedra to Romanticism. According to Valera, Saavedra was already Romantic before Malta without realizing it.

VAN TIEGHEM, PAUL. *Le romantisme dans la littérature européenne* (Paris: Albin Michel, 1948). One of the most valuable studies of European Romanticism; discusses Romanticism on an international scale. Somewhat external analysis, though such categories as "religion," "love," "exoticism," "historicism," etc., are discussed.

WELLEK, RENÉ. "The Concept of Romanticism in Literary History," in *Concepts of Criticism* (New Haven: Yale University Press, 1963). Insists on the basic unity of the Romantic movement throughout Europe.

————. "Romanticism Re-examined," in *Concepts of Criticism* (New Haven: Yale University Press, 1963). Invaluable assessment of critical works on this subject (1945–62).

Index

(The works of Rivas are listed under his name)

187